AMERICA HAS A BETTER TEAM

"I'm thrilled to see our story captured so well."

—LOU SPADIA,
Former president of the San Francisco 49ers

PUBLISHED IN SAN FRANCISCO

**HARBOR
PUBLISHING**

AMERICA

HAS

A BETTER

TEAM

THE STORY OF
BILL WALSH AND
SAN FRANCISCO'S
WORLD CHAMPION
49 ERS

GLENN DICKEY

INTRODUCTION BY
HERB CAEN
A TRIBUTE BY
MAYOR DIANNE FEINSTEIN

To Nancy and Scott, who have to put up with the absent-mindedness and grouchiness of a writer at work.

Cover & Design: Design Office
Manufacturing Coordination: Peter G. Levison
Production: BookPack, Inc.
Production Director: Ray Riegert
Editor: Sayre Van Young
Typesetting: Kay Murray-Nears, Allen Hayward, Diane Valay
Paste-up: Beee Langley, Phil Gardner
Proofreading: Leslie Henriques, Kris Johnson
Consultants: Bruce LoPucki, Sam Lawson
Text Printer/Binder: Publisher's Press
Mountain States Bindery
Photos © Michael Zagaris and Dennis Desprois

Paperback/ISBN 0-936602-47
Cloth/ISBN 0-936602-48-1
Limited Cloth/ISBN 0/936602-49

ACKNOWLEDGEMENTS

My thanks go to Bill Alexander and Jack Jennings of Harbor Publishing, who realized seconds after Dwight Clark caught Joe Montana's pass against Dallas that there had to be a book on the 49ers.

Although much of this book is based on my own recollections and conversations with players and coaches, I also relied on written accounts to fill in information gaps. In that regard, I found Ira Miller's stories in the *San Francisco Chronicle* of special value.

Finally, my gratitude goes to Lou Spadia, who not only supplied me with information but has also personified the special spirit of the 49ers for so many years.

1981 NFL STANDINGS

AMERICAN FOOTBALL CONFERENCE

Eastern Division

	W	L	T	PCT.	PTS.	OP
*Miami	11	4	1	.719	345	275
#NY Jets	10	5	1	.656	355	287
#Buffalo	10	6	0	.625	311	276
Baltimore	2	14	0	.125	259	533
New England	2	14	0	.125	322	370

Central Division

	W	L	T	PCT.	PTS.	OP
*Cincinnati	12	4	0	.750	421	304
Pittsburgh	8	8	0	.500	356	297
Houston	7	9	0	.438	281	355
Cleveland	5	11	0	.313	276	375

Western Division

	W	L	T	PCT.	PTS.	OP
*San Diego	10	6	0	.625	478	390
Denver	10	6	0	.625	321	289
Kansas City	9	7	0	.563	343	290
Oakland	7	9	0	.438	273	343
Seattle	6	10	0	.375	322	388

NATIONAL FOOTBALL CONFERENCE

Eastern Division

	W	L	T	PCT.	PTS.	OP
*Dallas	12	4	0	.750	367	277
#Philadelphia	10	6	0	.625	368	221
#NY Giants	9	7	0	.563	295	257
Washington	8	8	0	.500	347	349
St. Louis	7	9	0	.438	315	408

Central Division

	W	L	T	PCT.	PTS.	OP
*Tampa Bay	9	7	0	.563	315	268
Detroit	8	8	0	.500	397	322
Green Bay	8	8	0	.500	324	361
Minnesota	7	9	0	.438	325	369
Chicago	6	10	0	.375	253	324

Western Division

	W	L	T	PCT.	PTS.	OP
*San Francisco	13	3	0	.813	357	250
Atlanta	7	9	0	.438	426	355
Los Angeles	6	10	0	.375	303	351
New Orleans	4	12	0	.250	207	378

*Division Champion
#Wild Card for Playoffs
NOTE: San Diego won AFC Western title over Denver on the basis of a better division record (6-2 to 5-3).

AFC First Round Playoff
Buffalo 31, New York Jets 27

AFC Divisional Playoff
Cincinnati 28, Buffalo 21
San Diego 41, Miami 38

AFC Championship
Cincinnati 27, San Diego 7

NFC First Round Playoff
New York Giants 27, Philadelphia 21

NFC Divisional Playoff
San Francisco 38, New York Giants 24
Dallas 38, Tampa Bay 0

NFC Championship
San Francisco 28, Dallas 27

Super Bowl
San Francisco 26, Cincinnati 21

CONTENTS

NUMERICAL ROSTER

No.	Name	Pos.	Ht.	Wt.	Age	NFL Exp.	College
3	Jim Miller	P	5-11	183	24	2	Mississippi
7	Guy Benjamin	QB	6-3	210	26	4	Stanford
14	Ray Wersching	K	5-11	210	31	9	California
16	Joe Montana	QB	6-2	200	25	3	Notre Dame
20	Amos Lawrence	RB	5-10	179	23	R	North Carolina
21	Eric Wright	CB	6-1	180	22	R	Missouri
22	Dwight Hicks	S	6-1	189	25	3	Michigan
24	Rick Gervais	S	5-11	190	22	R	Stanford
27	Carlton Williamson	S	6-0	204	23	R	Pittsburgh
28	Lynn Thomas	CB	5-11	181	22	R	Pittsburgh
29	Saladin Martin	CB	6-1	180	25	2	San Diego State
30	Bill Ring	RB	5-10	215	25	1	Brigham Young
31	Walt Easley	FB	6-1	226	24	R	West Virginia
32	Ricky Patton	RB	5-11	192	27	4	Jackson State
35	Lenvil Elliott	RB	6-0	210	30	9	N.E. Missouri
38	Johnny Davis	RB	6-1	235	25	4	Alabama
42	Ronnie Lott	CB	6-0	199	22	R	USC
49	Earl Cooper	FB	6-2	227	24	2	Rice
51	Randy Cross	G	6-3	250	27	6	UCLA
52	Bobby Leopold	LB	6-1	215	24	2	Notre Dame
53	Milt McColl	LB	6-6	220	22	R	Stanford
54	Craig Puki	LB	6-1	231	24	2	Tennessee
56	Fred Quillan	C	6-5	260	25	4	Oregon
57	Dan Bunz	LB	6-4	225	26	4	Cal State-Long Beach
58	Keena Turner	LB	6-2	219	23	2	Purdue
59	Willie Harper	LB	6-2	215	31	8	Nebraska
60	John Choma	G-C	6-6	261	26	1	Virginia
61	Dan Audick	T	6-3	253	27	4	Hawaii
62	Walt Downing	C-G	6-3	254	25	4	Michigan
64	Jack Reynolds	LB	6-1	232	34	12	Tennessee
65	Lawrence Pillers	DE	6-4	260	29	6	Alcorn A & M
66	Allan Kennedy	T	6-7	275	23	R	Washington State
68	John Ayers	G	6-5	260	28	5	West Texas State
71	Keith Fahnhorst	T	6-6	263	29	8	Minnesota
74	Fred Dean	DE	6-2	230	29	7	Louisiana Tech
75	John Harty	DT	6-4	253	24	R	Iowa
76	Dwaine Board	DE	6-5	250	25	3	North Carolina A & T
78	Archie Reese	DT	6-3	262	25	4	Clemson
79	Jim Stuckey	DE	6-4	251	23	2	Clemson
80	Eason Ramson	TE	6-2	234	25	3	Washington State
84	Mike Shumann	WR	6-0	175	26	4	Florida State
85	Mike Wilson	WR	6-3	210	23	R	Washington State
86	Charle Young	TE	6-4	234	30	9	USC
87	Dwight Clark	WR	6-4	210	24	3	Clemson
88	Freddie Solomon	WR	5-11	185	28	7	Tampa

Injured Reserve: Ken Bungarda, Ricky Churchman, Phil Francis, Eric Herring, Paul Hofer, Pete Kugler, Ed Judie, Gus Parham, George Visger.

1981 RESULTS & ATTENDANCE

PRESEASON (2-2-0)

(W)	49ers	27	at Seattle	24	(OT)	56,958
(L)	49ers	28	San Diego	31		41,667
(W)	49ers	24	Seattle	17		37,563
(L)	49ers	7	at Oakland	21		51,192
TOTAL ATTENDANCE						187,380

REGULAR SEASON (13-3-0)

(L)	49ers	17	at Detroit	24	62,123
(W)	49ers	28	Chicago	17	49,520
(L)	49ers	17	at Atlanta	34	56,653
(W)	49ers	21	New Orleans	14	44.433
(W)	49ers	30	at Washington	17	51,843
(W)	49ers	45	Dallas	14	57,574
(W)	49ers	13	at Green Bay (Milw)	3	50,171
(W)	49ers	20	Los Angeles	17	59,190
(W)	49ers	17	at Pittsburgh	14	52,878
(W)	49ers	17	Atlanta	14	59,127
(L)	49ers	12	Cleveland	15	52,445
(W)	49ers	33	at Los Angeles	31	63,456
(W)	49ers	17	New York Giants	10	57,186
(W)	49ers	21	at Cincinnati	3	56,796
(W)	49ers	28	Houston	6	55,707
(W)	49ers	21	at New Orleans	17	43,639
TOTAL ATTENDANCE					872,741

POST SEASON (3-0-0)

(W)	49ers	38	New York Giants	24	58,360
(W)	49ers	28	Dallas	27	60,525
(W)	49ers	26	Cincinnati	21	

A TRIBUTE

BY MAYOR DIANNE FEINSTEIN

On January 25, 1982, San Francisco outdid herself in sheer jubilation. At least a half million persons jammed downtown to cheer the triumphant 49ers on their return from Super Bowl XVI. San Francisco had seen nothing like it in terms of massive numbers of joyous celebrants since V.J. Day at the end of World War II. Some say the crowd totaled a million shouting and waving 49er fans. The city's 49er fever climbed with mounting anticipation as the team won game after game in its most spectacular season. It reached a high point in the play-offs with a mighty and unforgettable leap by Dwight Clark to gather in the winning touchdown over Dallas. And, of course, it soared to its apex in the great victory in the Super Bowl.

The 49ers, defying all odds, and in a tradition typical of San Francisco herself, rebuilt from the ashes of past defeats. They did so with determination, extraordinary effort and a calm sense of confidence. Their indomitable spirit gives pride to us all.

On behalf of San Francisco, I thank the 49ers for giving this city a splendid sense of hope and accomplishment. America has a great team ... and it is ours.

INTRODUCTION

BY HERB CAEN

"The World Champion San Francisco 49ers!"

It does have a certain lilt, that phrase. Thousands of us never thought we'd live long enough to hear it. Even now, when the fact that we are paramount in the world of professional football has sunk in, we find it difficult to believe. There is a fictional quality about the whole thing, a football version of "Damn Yankees," with a guy named Joe coming from out of nowhere to lead a young band of comparative unknowns to glory in the snowy January fields of Michigan.

A trip to the moon on gossamer wings? No, better. A trip to Pontiac, Michigan, to the Super Bowl in the Silverdome, there to defeat the Cincinnati Bengals on a day that will join some of the other legendary dates in the long history of Baghdad-by-the-Bay — January 24, April 18, November 11, August 15.

Reading backward from the final date, those great days would be the end of World War II in 1945, Armistice Day in 1917, the Great Fire and Earthquake of 1906, and the discovery of gold in 1848.

By wonderful coincidence, the 49ers discovered gold in the Silverdome on the very same date 134 years later — January 24, 1982. A powerful omen, and there were others. Quarterback Joe Montana's number is 16, the Super Bowl victory was the sixteenth of the season for the 49ers, and the game itself was Super Bowl XVI.

Not only that, it had been exactly 49 days since the 49ers

had met the Bengals for the first time, during the regular season, and had trounced them.

The team is young, it is solid, it will be together for years to come. Therefore, it may not be too wildly optimistic to predict that a dynasty was born that wintry afternoon in the unlikely setting of a depressed auto-geared city 30 miles from Detroit. Last year, it was the Oakland Raiders who won it all, a dynasty that had run its course and now faces the slow, agonizing task of rebuilding. For Bay Area football fans, it has been a remarkable two years, with the promise of more golden years to come. Make that scarlet and gold, the 49er colors.

"O ye of little faith!" I will confess that I was one of those who had almost given up on the Niners. Unlike the 49er faithful, who have stayed gallantly with the team through thick and thin, I only stuck through the thick — the exciting first years of the team, when we called ourselves the student body of "49er U.," wouldn't dream of missing a Sunday at old Kezar Stadium, and looked upon surrounding Golden Gate Park as our campus.

We were young, the team was young, and quarterback Frankie Albert, the demon bootlegger and quick-kicker, the most exciting player we had ever seen. In fact, his refreshing ad lib style would be exciting today, but let us not get off the subject. The years of Albert, Norm Standlee, Johnny "Strike" Strzykalski, Leo Nomellini, Bob St. Clair, Billy Wilson, Gordy Saltau, Y. A. Tittle, Hugh McElhenney, Joe "The Jet" Perry are enshrined in the hearts of us oldsters as among the best years of our lives.

Kezar itself was a dump, a madhouse populated almost entirely by maniacs, and yet, like so many things about San Francisco, it had a certain tacky charm. The seats were benches. The knees of the people behind you were constantly in your back, as yours were in someone else's. The "facilities" were laughably primitive. The stadium even ran the wrong way — East and West, rather than North and South — because the legendary Super-intendent of the Park, "Uncle John" McLaren, who didn't want it there in the first place, insisted it be built in a manner that"would not disturb my beloved petunia beds."

Late in the fourth quarter, in came the fog and in came the sea gulls. If the day were clear, the sun would start setting just above the West rim of the stadium, driving the visiting quarterbacks and ends crazy. It was warm, corny, cozy, impossible and unforgettable — big league football in bush league surroundings, centered on a team of home-towners run by a home-town family, the Morabitos. We indentified like mad with those Niners.

When the team moved to Candlestick, some of us Original Faithful fell off the bandwagon, even though we admired the quarterbacking of John Brodie, the grace of Gene Washington, and, a bit later, the dramatic running of Paul Hofer. The seasons came and went, coaches came and went, new owners came, and a lot of us still went. "What have you done for the 49ers lately?" one asked me. "What have the 49ers done for me?" I replied after suffering through a couple of 2-14 seasons.

For a spell, the Niners became a joke. "They're called the 49ers because they never get beyond the 49-yard line. The original 49ers found gold, these guys can't even find the goal." We tried to be blasé about the whole thing. San Francisco is, after all, among the most sophisticated of cities. Unlike towns like Oakland, we said, we don't NEED winning football or baseball teams. We have the opera —in fact, we had the very best, Enrico Caruso, in 1906, when Cincinnati, the first major league baseball city, was a cow town.

We have culture, a major symphony and ballet, fine museums, incredible scenery, marvelous climate, the greatest pair of bridges, world-class restaurants and hotels — who cares if the Giants haven't been in the World Series since 1962, and that the 49ers haven't won a title in 36 years?

I remember writing something painfully lofty about "cities that have so little else going for them that they have to identify with their athletic teams. San Francisco doesn't need that. Our priorities are in line."

How wrong I was, and I suppose I knew it deep down inside all the time. The 49ers Super Bowl victory touched off the wildest, craziest demonstration since V-E Day, and the glow lives on. Some urban critics have called San Francisco "a city of losers," because of our high suicide rate and heavy drinking, and while these are still problems, that title now rings false. We still have major problems, to be sure, that a winning football team will never help to solve, but civic morale has been given a boost that makes San Franciscans feel a little prouder, a bit closer to one another.

The long era of "Wait till next year" is over.

The jokes have ended.

"The World Champion San Francisco 49ers!" are here to stay for a long time, and a new chapter in the ongoing story of Baghdad-by-the-Bay now begins.

HOW THE 1981 49ERS WERE BUILT

YEAR	NUMBER ACQUIRED	DRAFTED(21)	FREE AGENTS(17)	TRADES(7)
1973	(1)	Willie Harper (2)		
1974	(1)	Keith Fahnhorst (2A)		
1976	(2)	Randy Cross (2A) John Ayers (8)		
1977	(1)		Ray Wersching (FA '73 Chargers)	
1978	(5)	Dan Bunz (1B) Walt Downing (2) Archie Reese (5A) Fred Quillan (7)		1. Freddie Solomon (D2A '75 Dolphins)
1979	(6)	Joe Montana (3) Dwight Clark (10A)	Dwaine Board (D5 '79 Steelers) Lenvil Elliott (D10 '73 Bengals) Dwight Hicks (D6A '78 Lions) Eason Ramson (D12 '78 Packers)	
1980	(9)	Earl Cooper (1A) Jim Stuckey (1B) Keena Turner (2) Jim Miller (3A) Craig Puki (3B) Bobby Leopold (8)	Ricky Patton (D10 '78 Falcons) Lawrence Pillers (D11 '76 Jets)	2. Charle Young (D1 '73 Eagles)
1981	(20)	Ronnie Lott (1) John Harty (2A) Eric Wright (2B) Carlton Williamson (3) Lynn Thomas (5A)	John Choma (D5 '78 Chargers) Walt Easley Allan Kennedy (D10B '81 Redskins) Saladin Martin (FA '79 Giants) Milt McColl Rick Gervais Jack Reynolds (D1B '70 Rams) Bill Ring (FA '80 Steelers) Mike Shumann (FA '78 Dolphins) Mike Wilson (D9 '81 Cowboys)	3. Guy Benjamin (D2 '78 Dolphins) 4. Dan Audick (D4 '77 Steelers) 5. Johnny Davis (D2 '78 Buckaneers) 6. Amos Lawrence (D4A '81 Chargers) 7. Fred Dean (D2 '75 Chargers)

TRADES

1. Prior to '78 from Miami with Vern Roberson and two draft choices for Delvin Williams.
2. Prior to '80 for a 5th round draft choice in '83 from Los Angeles.
3. Prior to '81 from New Orleans for future undisclosed draft choice.
4. Prior to '81 for a 3rd round draft choice in '82 from San Diego.
5. Prior to '81 from Tampa Bay for James Owens.
6. Prior to second game of '81 for a 4th round draft choice in '84 from San Diego.
7. Prior to 5th game in '81 from San Diego for 2nd pick & option to exchange No. 1 picks in '83

1

A FRANCHISE IS BORN

As the San Francisco 49ers swept to their first Super Bowl ever, setting team records as they went, the entire Bay Area went 49er crazy. Songs were written about the team; bars sold exotic drinks for 49 cents; advertising campaigns for all kinds of products—T-shirts, cars, cameras, TVs—were linked with the 49ers. Posters, signs, and graffiti featuring team members suddenly appeared everywhere.

None of this was surprising, because the 49ers are an important part of the social and cultural environment of San Francisco. The 49ers *are* San Francisco, and vice versa.

For one thing, the team has never played anywhere else. The Chicago Bears started in Decatur, Illinois; the Green Bay Packers often play in Milwaukee; the New York Giants have played in Connecticut and New Jersey; the Los Angeles Rams started out in Cleveland and ended up in Anaheim.

But the 49ers have always played in San Francisco, first at Kezar and now at Candlestick Park, both stadiums unfortunate reminders of the city's inability to do anything quite right, a weakness of which residents are perversely proud.

The 49er name obviously recalls the well-known historic past of San Francisco. The team's initial logo—a drunken gold miner shooting off two pistols, one seemingly aimed at his head—is also a reminder of San Francisco's reputation as a town of serious drinkers.

"In the original picture," says Lou Spadia, who rose to

club president in the sixties, "there was a saloon in the background." The 49ers removed the saloon, but the image wasn't changed.

Until the 1981 season, the 49ers reflected San Francisco in yet another way: the club was usually entertaining but never entirely successful. In fact, all of the teams in the National Football League when the 49ers joined in 1950 won conference titles before the Niners finally did. Nine teams formed since 1950—Baltimore, Dallas, Denver, Kansas City, Miami, Minnesota, the New York Jets, Oakland, and San Diego—had won conference titles, while the 49ers struggled on.

In the late sixties, Spadia and Dick Berg, then the club's promotion director, coined the term "49er Faithful" to describe the fans who had stayed with the team through thick and mostly thin. The term had more and more of an ironic connotation as the frustrations continued on for the next decade.

The idea for a professional football team from San Francisco probably grew from a discussion in 1943 between businessman Tony Morabito and Bill Leiser, sports editor of the *San Francisco Chronicle*. Leiser told Morabito of Arch Ward's plan for a new football league to start after World War II. (Ward, the sports editor of the *Chicago Tribune*, originated both the baseball All-Star game and the NFL champions/College All-Stars game.)

Morabito, a self-made success who rose from an $80-a-month truck driver to become the owner of a successful lumberyard before he was 30, thought he saw the possibility of another financial bonanza with a local pro team. He reasoned that many of the servicemen passing through San Francisco, chief port of embarkation for the war in the Pacific, would later return as tourists or permanent residents, and would become enthusiastic football fans of a Bay Area team.

Leiser warned Morabito to be ready to lose a lot of money, at least at the start. Morabito, insisting he was prepared, soon proved his point. Though he originally made his partners in the lumberyard partners in the 49ers, when the 49ers opened in a bath of red ink, Morabito borrowed $100,000 to buy them out. For the next three decades, the 49ers would belong to the Morabito family—and friends.

Tony Morabito was an extraordinary man, with an emotional range that swept from love to hate and didn't miss any stops in between. To those he cared about, he was capable of almost unbelievably generous acts. He allowed his first quarterback, Frank Albert, and a friend, Franklin Mieuli, to buy parts of the club for nominal figures, an act which made both men wealthy in a fairly short period of time.

His treatment of Lou Spadia, who joined the club shortly after the end of World War II, was another prime example of Morabito's generosity. Spadia was doing a fine job for the 49ers. As a matter of fact, he was doing several — selling tickets, handling office paper work, acting as equipment manager. Morabito appreciated Spadia's hard work, and in time, gave Lou a chance to buy five percent of the club at considerably less than true value. It took a lot of scraping and borrowing, but Spadia managed it, and he held that stock until the DeBartolo family bought the club in 1977.

But to those he disliked, Morabito's anger could be awesome. Many of those he disliked were newspapermen. Many of those he liked were also newspapermen. Sometimes they were the same men—at different times.

Morabito had an ongoing feud with the San Francisco press. Though some feuds—such as the one he had with *San Francisco Examiner* sports editor Curley Grieve—were longstanding, most depended on what a writer had written that day. He had a list of writers who displeased him, and a writer could make a spectacular leap, from say tenth on the list to the top, with a particularly critical story.

But even those newspapermen who feuded with Morabito had many good times with Tony, and everybody who knew him grieved when he died of a heart attack during a 1957 game with the Chicago Bears. The players learned of his death at the start of the second half; behind 17-7 at the time, they played the last two quarters with an emotional fervor, tears running down the faces of many players, and turned the game around, winning 24-17. Afterwards, Frank Albert, then the coach, said, "If he was going to live, I would have been happy to lose by a hundred points."

* * * *

The San Francisco 49ers started play in 1946 in the new All-America Conference with one of the finest offensive teams ever, featuring Albert at quarterback, Norm Standlee at fullback, Alyn Beals at wide receiver, and John Strzykalski at halfback.

Their record in the AAC was excellent, too: 9-5, 8-4-2, 12-2, and 9-3, for an overall mark of 38-14-2. But they had the misfortune of being in the same league as the Cleveland Browns, then the best team in football. The Browns won the AAC championship four years running with the 49ers finishing second every time. In 1950, the Browns and 49ers were admitted into the established league; the Browns went on to win the NFL title.

The 49ers' move into the NFL was not as successful as the Browns: San Francisco finished 3-9 in its first NFL season. For the next three decades, the 49ers would field teams that were often entertaining — usually because of such offensive stars as Hugh McElhenny, Joe Perry, Y. A. Tittle, and John Brodie — but which had only occasional periods of success. And even the successful periods always ended in frustration.

There was, for instance, the 1957 season, for which the term "cliffhanger" could have been invented. Fooling around in practice, quarterback Tittle and wide receiver R. C. Owens developed the "Alley Oop" pass: Tittle would lob a high pass and Owens would use his great leaping ability (he had played basketball in college) to take the ball away from a defender. Done right, it was impossible to defend against.

Using the "Alley Oop" often in critical periods, the 49ers tied the Detroit Lions for the Western Conference title with an 8-4 record. In the playoff game, the 49ers led at halftime, 24-7, then surged to 27-7 with a field goal early in the third quarter.

And then they collapsed. The Lions stormed back to win the game, 31-27, and it would be 13 long years before the 49ers came close again. When they did—in the 1970-72 period—each season brought similar near-miss frustration.

The 1970 season was the best ever for the 49ers since joining the NFL: 10-3-1. They clinched the Western Division title with a smashing 38-7 win over their cross-Bay rivals, the Oakland Raiders. John Brodie was named Player of the Year, Dick Nolan Coach of the Year, and cornerback Bruce Taylor Rookie of the Year. But in the NFC championship game, the 49ers lost to the Dallas Cowboys, 17-10.

In 1971 the 49ers took another divisional title, this time with a 9-5 record. But for the second year in a row, in the NFC title game against the Cowboys, they were overrun 14-3.

In 1972 the persistent 49ers won their third straight division title only to be eliminated by Dallas in the first round of the playoffs, 30-28, perhaps an even more bitter defeat than to the Lions in 1957.

With 1:53 left in the game, the 49ers led Dallas, 28-16. Dick Berg, sitting in the stands with 30,000 buttons proclaiming "Super Bowl Fever," eagerly wanted to start distributing them.

"Not yet," said club president Spadia. "I remember 1957."

Dallas quarterback Roger Staubach took over for Craig

Morton and quickly threw a touchdown pass that brought the Cowboys close at 28-23.

On the ensuing kickoff, the Cowboys recovered an onside kick fumbled by Preston Riley (who never played another game for the 49ers). Again, Staubach took the Cowboys in for a touchdown, and the Niners were suddenly beaten.

That defeat seemed to take the heart out of the 49ers; next season they slipped to the bottom of their division with a 5-9 record.

The following dismal years — with 0-0 and 5-9 records—cost Nolan his job, and Monte Clark took over for the 1976 season.

Clark brought the 49ers back to a measure of respectability with an 8-6 record in 1976, narrowly missing the playoffs. But that decent year only set the stage for yet another incredible saga in the 49er story.

* * * *

After the death of Vic Morabito, Tony's brother, in 1963, the 49ers had been primarily owned by the Morabito widows, Jane and Jo.

Since the mid-seventies, the Morabito women had been anxious to sell the team. At one point, the club was almost bought by Wayne Valley, a former general partner of the Oakland Raiders who'd sold his Oakland interest because of a feud with Al Davis. In fact, Valley was so close to buying the Niners that Spadia had consulted with him before hiring Clark as coach.

But the ownership agreement for the 49ers included a provision which allowed minority owners a chance to buy the club before it could be offered to an outsider. Part-owner Mieuli tried to put together a deal, but it fell through. And by the time it did, Valley had lost interest, mainly because the asking price had risen from $12 million to $15 million.

It rose even further until the DeBartolo Corporation, for anywhere from $18 million to $23 million (depending on the accounting system used), bought ninety percent of the club. Mieuli retained his five percent, and Jane Morabito another five percent. Edward J. DeBartolo, Jr., was named owner, at 31 the youngest in the National Football League.

It was the end of an era, the first time the club had been owned by non—Bay Area residents.

Bay Area fans soon learned about the DeBartolo Corporation, founded in 1948 by Edward J. DeBartolo, Sr., and based in Youngstown, Ohio. It's the world's leading planner, builder, owner, and operator of regional shopping malls; the corporation also owns thoroughbred race tracks, hotels, industrial and executive office parks, a foreign trade zone and overseas shipping operation, the Pittsburgh Penguins hockey team, and the Pittsburgh Civic Arena. Net worth? It's estimated at between $750 million and $1 billion.

With the DeBartolos came Joe Thomas, a lifelong friend of Ed DeBartolo, Sr., and the man who had put the deal together—with the provision that he be named general manager.

Monte Clark, who had been an assistant coach at Miami when Thomas had been with the Dolphins, knew he couldn't work with Thomas; though offered a tax-sheltered $100,000 salary, he resigned.

Things didn't get better. Indeed, if Joe Thomas had drawn up a plan for disaster, he couldn't have done a more complete job with the 49ers. He did everything wrong.

Convinced that the San Francisco team needed to be completely rebuilt, he virtually gave away such quality veteran players as defensive end Tommy Hart and defensive back Mel Phillips. And his drafts were simply not good; not *one* player remains in the league from his first draft in 1977.

Trying to buy time, he traded for O.J. Simpson, whose legs were gone. O.J. did virtually nothing for the 49ers, but he cost the team second- and third-round picks in 1978 and a first-round pick in 1979—which turned out to be the very first pick in the draft that year.

Under Thomas's dismal misdirection, the 49ers went first to 5-9 and then to a league-worst 2-14. His first coach, Ken Meyer, was fired after one year. The second, Pete McCulley, lasted only nine games into the second season; then Fred O'Connor had a turn. It made no difference who coached; Thomas had all the authority. He cut the squad and told coaches who to play.

As the losses mounted, Thomas raged at the players, fuming into the dressing room to lecture them after losses. He fought with a sportswriter in a bar on a road trip. He alienated fans. When one fan put up a banner at Candlestick reading, "Blame Joe Thomas," Thomas had the guy ejected from the stadium. A group of fans formed an organization called "Doubting Thomases," with the express aim of getting rid of Thomas. It was a very ugly period in the history of the 49ers.

In the midst of all this, Edward DeBartolo, Jr., announced that Thomas's contract would be extended four years. It was a mistake, as DeBartolo admitted later, but an understandable one.

"I was looking for stability," he explained. "Because of all the turmoil, all the press criticism, I thought it was important to make a statement. If I had it to do all over again, if I could go back and think about it, no, I wouldn't have done it. I don't think now that it was the right thing to do."

DeBartolo's serious doubts about Thomas had begun before he made the contract announcement. "I hadn't really been happy about what was happening in the organization for several months." But he wanted to wait to make a final evaluation, without the emotion of the season intruding on his decision.

But when DeBartolo didn't sign the contract extension (the focal point of a later legal dispute with Thomas), Thomas knew he was in danger. Shortly thereafter, Thomas charged into the 49er dressing room after a loss to St. Louis and told the players, "If I'm going down the tubes, I'm going to take you with me."

He didn't last long enough to make good on his threat. DeBartolo fired him, less because of what the team was doing on the field than what was happening behind the scenes.

"Nobody felt at ease and comfortable within the organization," said DeBartolo. "*I* didn't even feel comfortable. You can't make an organization work that way."

One positive result came from the otherwise unpleasant situation: DeBartolo learned what he had to do. "I'm not afraid to admit I've made mistakes," he said, "but I think I've learned a lot."

He proved that with his next move: he named Stanford coach Bill Walsh as his new coach (and, a little later, general manager). Though it would take a couple of years for success, that decision started the 49ers on their way to the Super Bowl.

2

WALSH ARRIVES TO GREET DISASTER

In one way, Bill Walsh's career resembles a show business personality more than a football coach: he's an "overnight success" after more than 20 years of hard work in relative anonymity.

Like Vince Lombardi, Walsh didn't get a head coaching job above the prep level until he was 45, a damning indictment of the judgment of those who hire coaches. He was twice passed over in the sixties for a job he coveted, head coach at San Jose State, his alma mater.

Walsh was ready to quit football in 1968 when he went back to graduate school. In his spare time he coached the San Jose Apaches, a semi-pro team, and did well enough to catch the attention of the Cincinnati organization: he was hired the next year as an offensive coach for the Bengals.

At Cincinnati he coached a young Ken Anderson, an unknown from a small Midwestern college who become a star quarterback under Walsh's tutelage. It was widely expected that Walsh would become head coach when Paul Brown retired, but Brown passed over him to select Bill Johnson.

Walsh then left Cincinnati and went to San Diego, where he coached quarterback Dan Fouts to stardom. That, finally, got him his chance, and he was selected to coach Stanford in 1977; at 45, he was the oldest coach in the conference.

Two years later, after leading Stanford to successive bowl seasons, he was named coach of the San Francisco 49ers.

His failure to get a head coaching job much earlier in his career made him bitter at the time. Now, he is more philosophical. "This isn't like civil service," Walsh says. "You don't pass an examination to move up. As often as not, getting the right job is a matter of luck and timing.

"The NFL is opening up a lot now, but for a time, it was a very tight little circle. Jobs got passed around to the same people—and I wasn't one of those people."

Spending so much time in obscurity would have discouraged most men, killing their ambition. Men with the drive of Lombardi and Walsh only become more determined.

"I decided eventually that the way to succeed was to establish a reputation in one area," says Walsh, "and I did that with the pass offense, becoming known as the leading authority—or, at least, one of the best—in that field."

Now, Walsh feels that he benefited from all those years as an assistant, especially at Cincinnati under Brown, who he says had the most influence on his career.

"Paul and I are different men," says Walsh, "but I learned an awful lot from him. He thought of everything, to the point of determining where jocks should be hung. He told us, for instance, to always take ten minutes after a game before we talked to the press, so we could collect our thoughts and not just talk without thinking.

"I was determined that I was going to work as hard as I could at my job and not get in the business of campaigning for a head job and then being disappointed when I didn't get it. I feel I've improved as a coach just about every year. Certainly, I was a better coach my second year at Stanford than my first, and I think I've learned some things on the job with the 49ers, too."

The Stanford job made Walsh's reputation. After the first year, he was offered a multiyear contract (at $100,000 a year), to coach the Chicago Bears. He turned it down because he didn't want to go back to the Midwest. "I don't know why I even talked to them, when I knew I wouldn't take it," he says. "Sometimes you do things for your ego."

He also talked to the Los Angeles Rams, but Carroll Rosenbloom hired George Allen instead. Then, in one of the more bizarre NFL happenings, Allen was fired during the exhibition season. The episode worked out perfectly for the 49ers, however, because it meant Walsh was available the next year.

Those long years in the athletic wilderness had an effect on Walsh's personality. For sure, he is not at all the coaching stereotype of a bland, programmed man who talks only in jargon and cliches.

Walsh doesn't suffer fools gladly, and he admits that one of the hardest parts of his job is disguising his disdain for stupid questions, particularly those from television commentators. He has cut short post-game interviews for that very reason.

Walsh is a brilliant man, and he doesn't pretend otherwise. He is often impatient with those not quick enough to keep up with him, and his off-the-record comments about his coaching colleagues are candid and often caustic.

He has the politician's knack for manipulating large press conferences, often giving reporters good quotes, while revealing little of himself or his team. Walsh won't volunteer information at those sessions, and he'll answer questions only in the most literal sense. At the press conference announcing his selection as 49er coach, for instance, he was asked if he'd told Ed DeBartolo that he wouldn't come to the 49ers if Joe Thomas remained. He replied that Thomas's name had never been mentioned. That was literally true, but what he left unsaid was also true: he would never have worked for Thomas.

Because he's guarded in his comments to reporters he doesn't know or trust, Walsh is misjudged by many. One writer, for instance, wrote that Walsh's only interest seemed to be football. In fact he has many other interests, from travel to history. Last summer he sent me a copy of James Fallow's thought-provoking book *National Defense*. Needless to say, that isn't the kind of book most coaches read—unless they mistake it for a book on the Pittsburgh Steelers' game strategy.

Walsh took the job as 49er coach and general manager for three reasons: money, opportunity, and a break from recruiting.

Though no figure was ever released, Walsh's salary is probably triple what he was getting at Stanford, at least $150,000 a year. And, he has the chance to coach the best. "I felt I could be a better coach on the professional level than college," he says, a point he has certainly proved. Finally, there's no more recruiting. "I frankly don't know how much longer I could have done that. It was a lot harder the second year at Stanford than the first. It gets harder and harder, doing all that traveling."

Walsh stepped into a disaster. The 49ers resembled an expansion team after Joe Thomas's dismantling. Worse yet, Thomas, Monte Clark, and Dick Nolan had traded away an incredible number of draft choices. In the four-year period from 1976 to 1979, the 49ers traded away 20 picks! Sixteen of those came from the first five rounds, traditionally the basis for building a team. By 1980, not one of the players the 49ers received for those draft choices was still with the team.

For the morbidly curious, here's how the deals went:

—In 1976 the 49ers traded their own first and another first obtained from Houston for Vic Washington, plus Tom Owen, to New England for Jim Plunkett. Number three went to Dallas for Bob Hayes, who played one year. Number four went to the Giants for Norm Snead, a deal engineered by Dick Nolan the year before. The number five pick was traded for Al Chandler, a tight end who never played for the 49ers.

—In 1977 the first two picks went to New England as part of the Plunkett deal. Number three went to the Jets for defensive tackle Ed Galigher. Number five went to Buffalo for linebacker Dave Washington (a good deal, except that Thomas then traded away Washington!). Number eight went to Tampa Bay for offensive lineman Johnny Miller, who never played a regular season game for the Niners.

—In 1978 the 49ers lost their second- and third-round picks in the Simpson deal. Number five, and Tom Mitchell, went to Washington for wide receiver and punt returner Larry Jones. Number eight went to Washington for linebacker Joe Harris.

—By 1979 Thomas was gone, but his mark remained. The number one pick went to Buffalo in a continuation of the Simpson deal. Number three went to Seattle because of a trade Thomas had made for defensive back Bob Jury. Number four was also in the Simpson deal. Number eight went, because of another trade Thomas had made the year before, for offensive guard Steve Knutson of Green Bay.

It was a bleak picture, but Walsh had a long-range plan. The first element was to work on the players' confidence, and to show them that progress could be measured by something other than wins. At the start, it would have to be.

"Some people say a loss is a loss," Walsh said in training camp, "but I don't buy that. If I have to lose, I'd rather lose by one point than 30. I look for small things. I think it's better to have three goal-line stands, for instance, and then allow a score than to give up a touchdown on the first down. I think you have to look at this as a 16-game season that is followed by another 16-game season. You have to look for improvement."

That first year Walsh drafted for offensive help, figuring that he could install enough of an offense to partially compensate for defensive failings. Lacking his first-round pick, he went for James Owens on the second round. Owens had been a running back at UCLA but Walsh thought he could be turned into a wide receiver and that with his speed (Owens was a world-class hurdler), he would be the kind of deep threat that Cliff Branch was for the Oakland Raiders.

Owens, a disappointment, was eventually traded to Tampa Bay for fullback Johnny Davis two seasons later; but Walsh also drafted quarterback Joe Montana on the third round that year and wide receiver Dwight Clark on the tenth. That combination would eventually be a key factor in getting the 49ers to the Super Bowl.

Because San Francisco had the worst record in pro football, they got first crack at players released by other teams that first year Walsh headed the team.

And Walsh had a system for that, too. He would bring free agents into camp and work them out in a separate session at noon time. If he thought the new player was a significant improvement over what he already had in camp, he'd bring the player into regular drills. If not, he'd quickly let the player go.

Most of the players who came into camp that summer of 1979 never got past the first test. But occasionally, Walsh would come up with a gem: defensive end Dwaine Board and free safety Dwight Hicks both joined the 49ers that way.

The 49ers were an entertaining team in 1979, and quarterback Steve DeBerg set NFL records with most completions (347) and most attempts (578). But the Niners finished at 2-14 for the second straight season, a crushing disappointment to Walsh.

"I really thought we could come in and make a big difference that first year," he said later. "We had done it at Stanford."

What was the difference?

"In college you can literally outsmart people," he said. "We had nothing on defense at Stanford that first year, but we would load up against the run until we stopped that and force teams to throw the ball, and they were generally inept at that.

"And then when we played LSU in a bowl game, well, we were flabbergasted at the way they would telegraph their plays. They ran them the same way all the time, so we knew exactly what they would do.

"But you don't get that kind of break in the pro game. Teams don't give anything away, and when teams are physically superior to you, they just keep pounding away until you break."

Before the 1980 draft Walsh made two key decisions. The first was to trade his number one pick. The 49ers had the second pick, behind only Detroit, in the first round, and Walsh could have drafted BYU quarterback Marc Wilson, whom he liked. But the 49er coach felt he needed more help at other positions, and that it was better to get two quality athletes instead of one. He traded that pick to the New York Jets, who drafted Lam Jones with it, in exchange for the Jets' two first-round picks; Earl Cooper, a running back, and defensive lineman Jim Stuckey were selected with the picks from the Jets.

Walsh's second decision was even more important: he decided the 49ers had to build defensively first, and the next two drafts concentrated on defensive players. In 1980 he got Stuckey, linebackers Keena Turner, Craig Puki, and Bobby Leopold, strong safety Ricky Churchman, and punter Jim Miller.

The 49ers still had some conspicuous weaknesses— sensitive people covered their eyes when the 49ers secondary tried to defend against a pass—but the improvement that Walsh was looking for was there.

Before the start of his second season, Walsh approved the slogan "Roaring Back," knowing full well that he would look ridiculous if the 49ers stumbled again. "I thought it'd be good for the players to have something to point for," he said. "Still, I thought of 'Roaring Back' as maybe something like 8-8. I didn't think we'd be in the Super Bowl."

The 49ers might even have reached Walsh's modest second-year goal. They started out well, taking three out of four exhibition games, including a whopping 33-14 win over the Oakland Raiders, who would go on to win Super Bowl XV. They won their first three games of the regular season, from New Orleans, St. Louis, and the New York Jets.

But in that third win, Dwaine Board was injured and declared out for the season. "I would rather have lost the game and kept Board," Walsh told me the next day. He knew, with Board gone, that the 49er pass rush would disappear, and the weak secondary would be exposed.

Atlanta ended the 49ers' three-game streak with a 20-17 win the next week, and then Los Angeles thrashed the Niners, 48-26. The worst was yet to come: Dallas totally manhandled the 49ers, 59-14, the next week, and running back Paul Hofer was knocked out for the season with a knee injury. Hofer had been the 49ers' primary offensive threat with his running and pass catching. Walsh called Hofer and Board his two best athletes, and in the span of three weeks, both had been lost.

Without Board and Hofer, the 49er season was doomed. They went on to lose eight in a row before finally beating the New York Giants, 12-0, in the twelfth game of the season. They finished the year at 6-10, a big improvement over the consecutive 2-14 seasons but hardly what the Faithful had expected when the team got off to a 3-0 start.

Still, there were some positive signs, and it didn't take a lot of searching to find them. For starters, Joe Montana had emerged as the number one quarterback, which pleased Walsh; he hadn't been sure Montana could develop that rapidly in only his second pro season.

DeBerg had a good arm and grasped Walsh's complex system well, but he wasn't mobile enough to scramble out of trouble. Worse, he had a tendency to throw critical interceptions, a fatal flaw for the 49ers because Walsh's system is based on controlling the ball through passing. All his quarterbacks—Ken Anderson and Dan Fouts in the pros, Guy Benjamin and Steve Dils at Stanford—had been taught not to throw high-risk passes. DeBerg could not seem to learn that lesson.

Montana, by contrast, was cool under pressure, probably because he had played at Notre Dame, where the pressure is always on. He seldom threw the pass interception which took the 49ers out of a game. Moreover, his mobility enabled him to gain a second or two of extra time, often enough to complete a pass.

Another positive sign that year was the 49ers rebounding in the homestretch of the season. Though they had nothing particularly to gain, they won three of their last five games.

One of their successes came against a potential playoff team, New England. The 49ers' 21-17 win knocked the Patriots out of playoff consideration and was the first time under Walsh that they had beaten a winning team.

The 49ers also nearly beat another playoff team, going down to the wire on a muddy, miserable day that ended the season before losing to Buffalo, 18-13.

But perhaps the most significant game of all was the fourteenth of the season, against New Orleans at Candlestick. The 49ers were trailing, 35-7, at halftime and seemed well on their way to one of the worst shellackings in their history. Instead, they pulled themselves together to outscore the Saints, 28-0, in the second half; in overtime, a Ray Wersching field goal beat New Orleans, 38-35, in what is officially termed the best comeback in NFL history.

That kind of character would make the 49ers champions in 1981.

3

HOW DO ROOKIES GET SO SMART?

Perhaps it was an omen when the 49ers were able to draft Ronnie Lott in the spring of 1981.

Bill Walsh had had no trouble identifying the area to strengthen for the 1981 season—the defensive backfield. It was just as easy to identify the backs who could help him: USC's Lott or UCLA free safety Ken Easley. Easley had the greater collegiate reputation, but given the choice, Walsh wanted Lott because the former Trojan could switch from his collegiate safety position to cornerback, the 49ers' weakest position.

But it seemed both Lott and Easley would be drafted before the 49ers' chance came up. Easley's agent tried to discourage other teams from drafting Ken by sending out letters saying he wanted to play in San Francisco and wouldn't report to another team. The tactic didn't work; Easley was drafted by the Seattle Seahawks.

That left only Lott, and Tampa Bay would probably pick him, just ahead of the 49ers. But the St. Louis Cardinals, expected to draft Pittsburgh's Hugh Green, surprised everybody by picking Alabama linebacker E.J. Junior. That left Green on the board, and Tampa Bay grabbed him.

Almost immediately, the 49ers announced they would draft Lott.

That was just one of two key moves the 49ers made in the off-season. The other was the acquisition of Jack Reynolds, a 34-year-old middle linebacker.

Reynolds had been a great player for the Los Angeles Rams, appearing in the Pro Bowl as late as January 1981, but the Rams had become disenchanted with him. They considered him a liability on pass defense because he'd lost a step of speed; Reynolds came off the field in obvious passing situations. He was also asking more money than they wanted to pay, and so the Rams released him. Very soon, the 49ers signed Reynolds as a free agent.

"A lot of us thought that was a mistake," said John Ralston, then working in the front office. "We figured we were building with youth, and what did we need with a 34-year-old linebacker? But, we were wrong, and Bill was right. Reynolds gave the team just what they needed in certain areas."

Certainly Reynold's physical ability alone was a plus. A sure, punishing tackler, he led the team in the 1981 season with 117 tackles, 28 more than any other player.

His attitude, though, was even more important. He looked at game movies almost more than the coaches, taking home reels of film to run on his own projector. His experience enabled him to position the 49ers perfectly on the field, and he acted almost as a coach with the younger players. His enthusiasm rubbed off on the others. "He's our Pete Rose," said Walsh.

As he had in 1980, Walsh concentrated on defensive help from the 1981 draft. (Incidentally, Walsh depends heavily on draft information supplied by John McVay, director of football operations, and college scouting director Tony Razzano and his scouts, but the final decision on who to pick is Walsh's.)

The first five picks in the draft—and six of the first seven—were defensive players. Four of the first five picks were defensive backs: Lott, Eric Wright, Carlton Williamson, and Lynn Thomas. "We didn't think there would be any good defensive backs coming out for the 1982 draft," explained Razzano, "so we had to get everything we could out of this draft."

The rookie defensive backs didn't have the luxury of a gradual break-in. Walsh started Lott, Wright, and Williamson from the beginning, though Lott's debut was delayed somewhat because he didn't sign until after the start of training camp. Moreover, Walsh declared that he expected the defensive backfield to be "the strongest part of our team."

Others scoffed. Newspaper writers were quick to point out that, in the first two exhibition games, the rookie backs played so far off the receivers (to prevent deep passes) that they couldn't defend against short- and medium-range passes. Defensive coordinator Chuck Studley, who had been an assistant with Walsh in Cincinnati, admitted he was "scared to death" at the idea of starting three rookies (four when Thomas was used in a five-back formation in obvious passing situations). Studley tried to make the rookie backs less vulnerable by dropping linebackers in pass coverage on every play, instead of using them to occasionally blitz.

But Walsh was proved right. The rookies played so much that they gained experience far more quickly than they would have normally. By the time the season was one-third over they were playing like veterans and, yes, the defensive secondary was the 49ers strongest point.

The exhibition season generally pleased Walsh. Though he, like everybody else, was concerned about a weakness at running back, he was encouraged by the great improvement on defense. That, in turn, took pressure off the offense because the 49ers didn't necessarily have to score five touchdowns to win a game.

Walsh knows, as do all followers of the game, that though you can compensate somewhat for your offensive weaknesses, the opposing offense, because it starts the play, can always find a defensive weakness.

"We've got nine good linebackers in camp and will only keep seven," noted Walsh. "We've got eight good linemen and can only keep six. For the first time, we're letting players go who could play somewhere else."

Because of travel costs, the 49ers confined their 1981 exhibition season to the West Coast, playing Seattle twice, San Diego, and Oakland. Walsh was pleased when his team beat Seattle twice.

"You have to remember that they humiliated us just two years ago [a 55-20 Seattle triumph]," he said. "This shows our progression—and, to be honest, their regression."

But unfortunately what impressed most people was the 49ers' 21-7 loss to the Raiders in the final exhibition game. The 49ers seemed inept on offense against the reigning World Champions. Walsh insisted that he had seen some positive aspects to the game, obviously referring to the defense. One columnist, though, thought Walsh had "flipped his noodle."

* * * *

In the first four games of the regular season, the 49ers played much as they had during the exhibition season, showing flashes of brilliant play but never displaying the consistency a champion needs.

Their first game was in the Silverdome in Pontiac, and the Niners gave no sign that they would be returning four-and-a-half months later for the Super Bowl. Billy Sims scored a touchdown with just 18 seconds remaining to give the Detroit Lions a 24-17 win in a game filled with errors by both sides.

Paul Hofer didn't play because Walsh didn't want to risk Hofer's knee on the artificial surface. (As it would turn out, Hofer played little all year and eventually re-injured his knee, apparently ending his career.)

To partially compensate, Walsh used ten varied backfield combinations, including one fullback and three wide receivers, and three running backs with two tight ends. Nothing worked very well.

The 49ers bounced back to beat the Chicago Bears, 28-17, in their home opener at Candlestick. Joe Montana had his best game yet, completing 20 of 32 passes for 287 yards without an interception, and throwing three touchdown passes.

The game was as much a Chicago loss as a San Francisco win, though. Walter Payton lost two fumbles and his team made so many errors that Bear coach Neill Armstrong lamented, "We saw ourselves self-destruct."

Happily for 49er fans it was the other team that beat itself this time, but that pleasant feeling lasted only until the following Sunday when the Falcons demolished the 49ers, 34-17, in Atlanta.

The game, even more lopsided than the score, was a particularly painful loss to Walsh because the many 49er errors—including a Montana interception returned 101 yards for a touchdown by Atlanta's Tom Pridemore—were reminiscent of the bad play of the seasons before. "We're too good a team to play like that," said Walsh.

The loss was especially painful because the obvious difference between the teams at that point was in the running offense. As the *Chronicle's* Ira Miller, the most knowledgeable of Bay Area pro football writers, pointed out, the 49ers could have drafted either or both of the Falcon running backs, William Andrews and Lynn Cain.

Again, the 49ers bounced back the next week to even their record with a 21-14 win over New Orleans at Candlestick. But again, the win came less from what the 49ers did than from what the other team failed to do.

The Saints outgained the 49ers by 99 yards, but one receiver, Rich Caster, dropped a pass in the end zone when no one was near him. Another receiver, Wes Chandler, tipped a pass

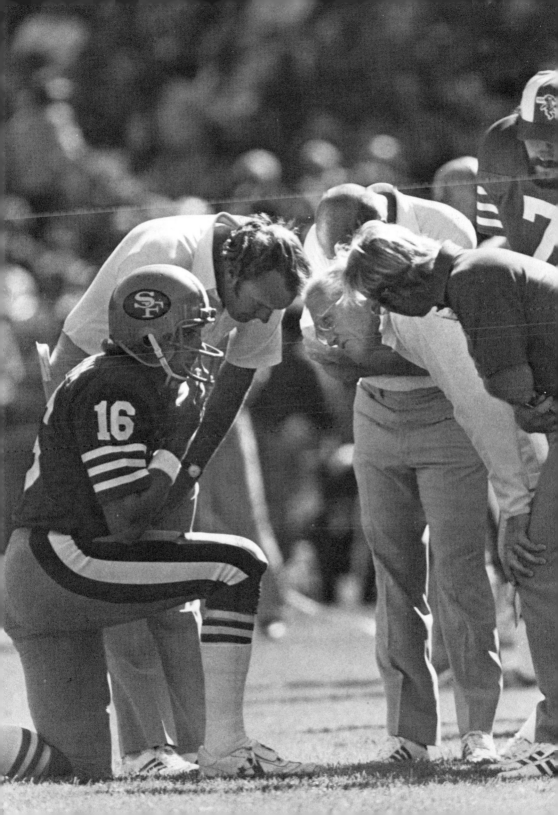

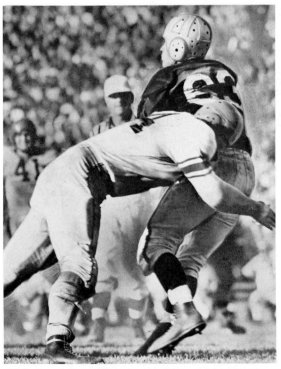

(overleaf) Joe Montana huddles with coaches as reserve quarterback Guy Benjamin listens. Hugh McElhenny, shown about to stiff-arm a would-be tackler, and John Brodie (above), fueled the high-powered offense in the 50s and 60s. Frankie Albert, hit by a Cleveland lineman just after releasing a pass, was the star of the first 49er team. Tony Morabito founded the 49ers and owned them until 1957. Joe Thomas (upper right) almost ruined the 49ers during his two years as general manager in 1977 and 1978. Monte Clark (bottom right) brought an interlude of success in 1976.

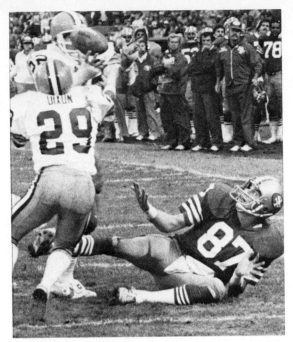

(top left) Dwight Clark slips and falls, and then watches helplessly as Joe Montana pass that was intended for him is intercepted in Cleveland game. The 49ers were driving toward what would have been a clinching touchdown before this play. They wound up losing to the Browns, their only loss in the last 15 regular season and playoff games.
(bottom left) Freddie Solomon shows the fine art of pass catching as he catches a ball with the fingertips of one hand behind the Dallas defense in the NFC championship game.
(right) Dallas defensive end Ed Jones stretches out to an eight-foot plus barricade, showing why he is nicknamed "Too Tall Jones" in the NFC championship game, but somehow, 49er quarterback Joe Montana gets the pass by Jones for an important completion.

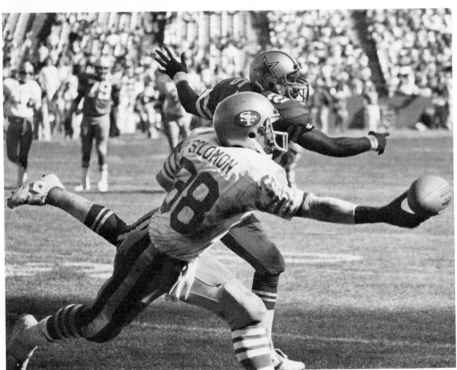

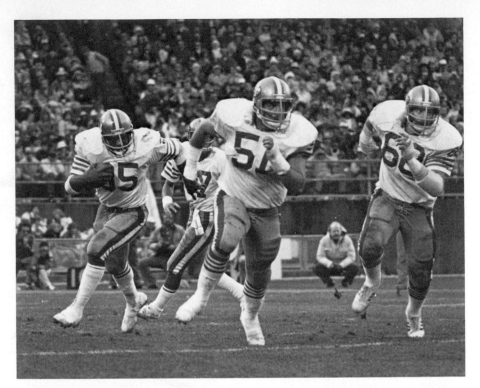

(top left) Pulling guards Randy Cross (51) and John Ayers (68) lead Lenvil Elliott around the right side against the New York Giants in the playoff game. (bottom left) Ricky Patton slips through hole created by blocking of Keith Fahnhorst (71 on left), Fred Quillan (on ground) and Johnny Davis (on right) in Houston win. (right) Dwight Clark and Raider defensive back Ted Watts reach for long pass, and Raider safety Burgess Owens also tries.

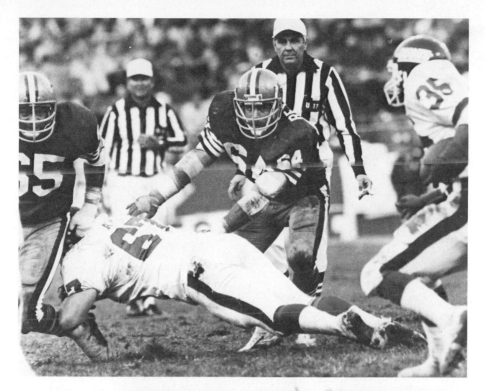

(left) Defensive end Fred Dean brings down Los Angeles running back Mike Guman after a short gain in second game, won by the 49ers, 33-31. (top right) 49ers middle linebacker Jack Reynolds pushes by a defender to make a tackle against the Giants in title-clinching victory. (bottom right) Ronnie Lott shows why the 49ers made him their No. 1 draft pick with this spectacular interception while falling.

(left) 49er tight end Charle Young and the Ram's Nolan Cromwell battle for a Joe Montana pass. (top right) Another look at Young as he signs autographs in the Candlestick parking lot after a 49er win. (bottom right) Paul Hofer slants through a good hole in the Atlanta defense as defensive back Tom Pridemore comes up to make the tackle.

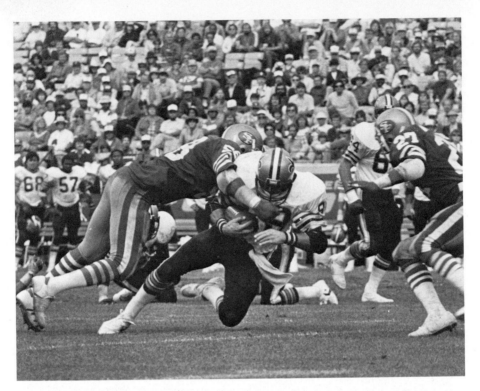

(top left) Keena Turner brings down an Atlanta runner as
Carlton Williams prepares to help. (bottom left) John Ayers,
his cheeks puffed out, shows the 49er intensity as he prepares
to block a Bengal defender in 21-3 regular season win over
Cincinnati. (right) Unofficial 49er cheerleader Wayne Tarr,
dressed appropriately for the Christmas season, prepares to
lead the 49er fans in a cheer during the Houston game, last of
the regular season home games.

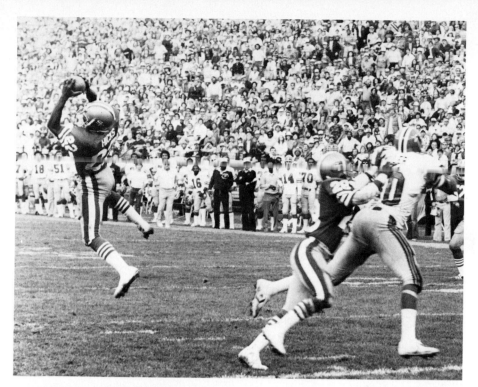

(left) Earl Cooper, who led the NFC in pass receiving in the 1980 season, shows why as he prepares to haul in a Joe Montana pass. (top right) Dwight Hicks leaps high to make an interception against Atlanta, as Lynn Thomas (28) prepares to defend the pass that never got that far. (bottom right) Dan Bunz draws a bead on Pittsburgh running back Frank Pollard.

that was intercepted by Ronnie Lott and returned for a touchdown. "That was a 'gimme'," said Lott after the game, and much the same could be said for the 49ers win.

Walsh had enjoyed a largely admiring press for his first two seasons, but some writers were beginning to criticize him at this point, which he felt unfair.

"I thought we had shown definite improvement," he said later. "We had won three of our last five games in the previous year, we were 2-2 in the exhibition season and barely lost one of those games to San Diego, in the last minute. The worst we were in the regular season was 1-2, so we weren't playing bad football.

"But I kept hearing how dull we were, and I knew some people were licking their chops, ready for us to fall. If we had, if the players had become disheartened by criticism, I don't know where we would have gone from there.

"I thought to myself, 'Give us a chance. Give this city a chance. San Francisco needs a team it can be proud of. Don't tear us down.' "

Very soon, though, his worries would be erased. The 49er season was about to turn around for two reasons: Fred Dean and the game against the Washington Redskins.

Dean had been a Pro Bowl defensive end for the San Diego Chargers, a fearsome pass rusher who helped disguise the Chargers' weakness in the defensive secondary. But he had been locked into a contract that just didn't compensate him fairly for his ability, and he finally refused to play for the Chargers any more.

The 49ers obtained him for a second-round draft choice in 1983, and the option of exchanging first-round positions in 1983. "NFL games are often won with a fourth-quarter pass rush," said Walsh. "That's where Dean is so valuable. If you're protecting a lead and the other team has to throw, he's all over the quarterback."

Dean reported to the 49ers but, because it took some time to work out his contract, didn't play in the next game against the Redskins. He would prove to be a very valuable addition in the weeks to come, but he wasn't needed in this one.

The 49ers simply smashed the Redskins, 30-17; at one point, they were up, 30-3. This was easily their most impressive victory of the season so far, especially since it happened on the road, where the 49ers had lost 26 of their previous 28 games.

The defense played especially well, and Dwight Hicks became the first 49er defensive player to score two touchdowns. In fact, Hicks, outgained the running backs and receivers on both sides of the field with 184 yards on two interception returns and a fumble recovery and run.

The loss dropped the Redskins to 0-5, and it seemed the 49ers had just beaten another bad team. But the Skins were a much better team than their record (which they proved by going 6-5 after that terrible start), and Walsh later regarded that game as the key to the 49er season.

"Washington had been moving the ball well all season [they were leading the NFC in yardage at the time]," said Walsh, "but they had been beating themselves with mistakes. It seemed they were about to break out.

"The attitude of the Washington media that week was, 'Now we've got a team we can beat.' We were playing on the road, in a hostile atmosphere. Then, we came out and just blitzed them! It was a real maturing process for the team."

All of which was fine for the moment, but the next week the 49ers would tangle with the Dallas Cowboys at Candlestick. The last time the teams had met, the Cowboys had won, 59-14. And that would be only the start of the toughest stretch of the 49ers schedule: in a seven-week span they had to play Dallas, Los Angeles twice, Atlanta, Pittsburgh, and Cleveland. Ouch!

4

DOOMSDAY FOR DALLAS

As usual, Bill Walsh was guarded in his comments at the press conference before the Dallas game. He described the Cowboys as a great team, certainly no exaggeration, and implied that his team was not yet in that class. "Are you suprised that you're 3-2?" asked one writer. "No," said Walsh. "We're good enough for that and we've played well enough to be 3-2. I would be surprised if we were 5-0."

When I talked to him later in his office, he was considerably less circumspect. I asked if he seriously thought his team could beat the Cowboys. "Yes," he said. "The one thing we [the coaches] have to worry about is that we don't start worrying about having to out-think the Cowboys. We're good enough now to stay with them physically."

The players, too, were confident. The atmosphere in the dressing room before the game was quiet and relaxed. Offensive tackle Keith Fahnhorst, who had been through the bad years, could spot the difference now. "We all felt we were going to win," he said.

The fans were ready, too. The game was a sellout, and the fans came early and stayed late.

They saw a game that some thought might have been the biggest victory in the history of the franchise; certainly it was the biggest to date under Walsh. The 49ers not only won the game, they dominated in every aspect.

The 49ers took command from the start, driving 61 yards

for a touchdown after the opening kickoff, with Joe Montana passing to Fred Solomon for the score.

When the 49ers got the ball back after a punt, they went 68 yards for another touchdown. This time Paul Hofer went in from four yards out. Hofer wound up as the 49ers leading rusher for the day with 40 yards on 11 carries.

Solomon figured in two key plays on this drive. On the first, he hit Dwight Clark for 25 yards on a pass off a threatened reverse. Solomon had been a quarterback in college and, though he couldn't pass well enough to be a pro quarterback, his ability was a genuine plus on a play like this.

Freddie was at the other end of a key pass later in the drive, when Montana scrambled away from a blitz and hit Solomon for 26 yards.

Still in the first period, the 49ers scored yet again. This time, the Cowboys were on the three after a San Francisco punt, and Jim Stuckey tackled Dorsett for a two-yard loss on first down. Then one play later, the 49ers got their only real break. Danny White passed to Drew Pearson, who fumbled at the six. The ball would have gone out of bounds but it hit the foot of line judge Dick McKenzie on the sideline and bounced to the 49ers Ronnie Lott, who recovered on the four. Four plays later, Johnny Davis scored from the one.

That made it 21-0 at the end of the first quarter, and the fans gave the home team a standing ovation as they changed ends of the field. The Niners went up 24-0 on a Ray Wersching field goal in the second quarter; finally the Cowboys scored, to make it 24-7 at halftime.

Now the 49ers had only one worry: that they would relax and the Cowboys would come back.

"After the Washington game," said Fahnhorst, "Hacksaw [Jack Reynolds] and I agreed that we've got to learn to bury a team when we've got a chance to. We can't let up."

On the second possession of the second half, the 49ers showed they had learned their lesson well. Clark took a ten-yard pass from Montana on the right sideline, made a move to get away from rookie cornerback Eversen Walls, and then beat safety Michael Downs and linebacker D.D. Lewis to the end zone for a 78-yard touchdown.

And the 49ers weren't through. Two plays after the ensuing kickoff, Lott returned an interception 41 yards for still another score. Wersching's kick made it 38-7 and the 49ers were coasting to their eventual 45-14 win.

After Lott's touchdown, Dallas coach Tom Landry took

quarterback Danny White out of the game to avoid the chance of injury at a meaningless point. Landry had conceded.

Actually, Landry had virtually given up much earlier. Asked after the game if he had thought the Cowboys would come back in the second half, Landry shook his head. "Most games that start out that way," he said, "end up as lopsided games, if you're playing a good team. The 49ers are a good team."

The details from that game are incredible. The first two times the Cowboys had the ball, they ran off three plays and had to punt. The third time, White fumbled on second down. The fourth time, Lott intercepted a pass on first down.

The 49ers led by 24-0 before the Cowboys even made a first down! Dallas crossed the 50-yard line only once in its first 13 possessions. Tony Dorsett, the league's leading rusher at the time, was held to 21 yards in nine carries, third lowest total of his five-year career; that game probably cost Dorsett the NFC rushing title. White passed for only 60 yards before he came out.

Walsh had worried about trying to outthink the Cowboys, using trick plays, but it was the Cowboys who had to resort to a flea-flicker and an end-around in desperation.

The statistics reflected the lopsidedness of the game: the 49ers had 23 first downs to 10, ran 80 plays to 53, and they gained 440 yards to only 192 for Dallas.

It was the biggest winning margin for the 49ers since 1974, when they had beaten Chicago 34-0, and the Cowboys' biggest losing margin since 1970.

There was no question that the 49ers had caught the Cowboys on one of those low days they sometimes experience during a season—nobody, after all, is really 31 points better than Dallas—but that didn't alter the significance of the win. In some games young teams find themselves, discovering just how good they can be, and the Dallas game was exactly that for the 49ers.

Nor was it a fluke. The 49ers won with good, solid football on both sides of the scrimmage line, and the only real break they got was the recovered fumble before their third touchdown. Considering their dominance throughout the game, and the score, it's hard to see how that fumble had much effect on the outcome.

"The thing a lot of people forget about Bill Walsh," CBS commentator and former coach Hank Stram told me later, "is that he's a sound fundamental coach."

"Since the rules have been relaxed to help the offense, a lot of coaches have opened up their offenses to take advantage of that, but they forget that their teams still have to block and tackle well. Walsh has never forgotten that, and that's been an important difference for him."

Probably the most encouraging aspect of the Dallas win was the dominance of the 49er defense, which really came together against a great team. Dean's presence made a big difference. He sacked White three times in the first half alone; for the game, he had four sacks. The first time the 49ers unveiled their new 4-2-5 defense with Dean, he sacked White.

Dean was so overwhelming in his first 49er game that he forced a change in the thinking of defensive coordinator Chuck Studley.

The basic 49er defense had been the 3-4, in which the defensive linemen are primarily expected to hold their ground; linebackers make most of the tackles. Former 49er defensive end Cedrick Hardman, who dislikes the 3-4 defense intensely, told me one time, "You need Clydesdales for that formation."

Hardman obviously regarded himself as a thoroughbred. Dean is too, and Studley didn't use him in the 3-4. Dean played only when the 49ers went to a 4-3, or any other defense aimed primarily at stopping the pass. When Studley saw how effective Dean was, he modified his defensive strategy to include more 4-3 defenses, giving Dean more opportunity to play.

Dean is incredible. He's so quick off the ball, it sometimes seems he's offside! Although only 228 pounds, he has enormous upper body strength and can't be manhandled by the largest of offensive linemen. Basically, he combines the quickness of a linebacker with the strength of a lineman.

His muscles come naturally, from a youth spent doing heavy manual labor. He shuns even the normal exercises done by players. "Any time I think of doing exercises," he explained, "I lie down until the feeling goes away."

Even without Dean, the 49er secondary had been playing very well. With him harassing and sacking the quarterback, the secondary became awesome, especially Ronnie Lott.

The rookie cornerback, who played safety when the 49ers added a fifth defensive back in passing situations, was playing an aggressive defense, staying tight on his man to break up passes or make interceptions and tackling with an awesome ferocity if the receiver did catch the ball.

As the 49ers knew when they drafted him, Lott is a super athlete. In high school he played shortstop on the baseball team and point guard on the basketball team, and in the one year (his junior year) he played basketball at USC, he made the varsity.

In high school, he was strictly an offensive player, first as wide receiver and then quarterback. He didn't play defensive back until he came to USC, but his background on offense has probably helped make him a defensive star. He's the right man in the right place at the right time.

The rule changes in 1978 in the NFL, forbidding defensive backs to bump a receiver more than once and allowing offensive linemen to use their hands in blocking, opened up the pass offense (which was, of course, the intent) and drove a lot of defensive coaches and defensive backs crazy. Speed and athletic ability became far more important than strength; the rule changes have forced an attitude change, too. Defensive backs can't play passively. They must be aggressive, willing to give up an occasional touchdown in exchange for a gambling, critical interception that can turn the game around. That's exactly the way Lott plays.

"Look," he says, using a colorful analogy, "we're playing with a loaded revolver back there, but you got to keep reloading it and play the game. If you don't, somebody's going to reload it for you and put bullets in all six chambers of that sucker, and it's going to go off all the time. I think defensive backs are starting to do that. I think the trend is starting to turn."

Meanwhile, Lott was receiving the ultimate compliment: opposing teams were throwing mainly to the other side, no longer willing to risk many passes on his side. That put more pressure on Eric Wright, the other rookie corner, but Wright was playing well, too, though not quite at the same level as Lott.

The decisive win over Dallas also showed the maturing of quarterback Montana and wide receiver Solomon.

Montana had been consistently downgraded by many in pro football, supposedly because he lacked a strong arm. To Walsh, that was nonsense.

"I can't find any negatives about Joe Montana's arm," he said. "People who say it's only an average arm are mistaken, and they always will be. Because his delivery is not a flick of the wrist like Terry Bradshaw's, they think it's not strong.

"He throws on the run while avoiding a pass rush, and he doesn't have to be totally set. He's not a moving platform like some others who are mechanical and can only do well when everything is just right. Joe performs just as well under stress."

Montana showed what Walsh meant against the Cowboys, completing 19 of 29 passes for 279 yards and two touchdowns, and consistently making the big play.

He was helped by an outstanding performance from the 49er offensive line, particularly Fahnhorst, who blocked Ed (Too

Tall) Jones so effectively that Jones might as well have stayed in Dallas. But even when Montana was under pressure, he often scrambled out of trouble to pass for an important completion.

Solomon, who caught his fifth touchdown in six games, joined the 49ers (in a trade by Joe Thomas) before the 1978 season; he came with a reputation for great talent but no discipline. At the back of his mind, he still thought he could play quarterback and sulked because nobody else agreed. In a game late in the disastrous 1978 season, Solomon got his chance when both 49er quarterbacks were hurt in the game. That humbling experience finally convinced him he belonged at wide receiver, and his improvement dated from that point.

Even so, in Walsh's first year Solomon made some spectacular plays but wasn't a dependable performer. When the 49ers needed a big catch late in the game, he wasn't the one to make it.

By 1981 that had changed. He was making big plays consistently. "He should be in the Pro Bowl," said Walsh. As late as 1979, Solomon was taking snaps from the center in practice so he could play quarterback in a pinch. No longer; he was too valuable now for Walsh to even consider a switch.

The stunning Dallas win should have established the 49ers among the NFL's elite, but there were still doubters. The 49ers hadn't been featured on Monday Night Football since 1977, and ABC producer Bob Goodrich made the decision not to show any plays from the 49er-Cowboys game on the halftime highlights. Of course, the fact that Los Angeles and Dallas were meeting in a special Sunday night game the next week, and that the 49er win would take some gloss off the Cowboys, was purely coincidental. Of course.

Walsh blasted that decision at his Tuesday press conference. "We're not accepted nationally, obviously," he said.

"The football elitists, jockstrap elitists don't consider us in the comfort zone. There are power sources, influence sources in the National Football League, 45-year-old men who are football groupies who prefer that we not exist so they can hold on to their football contracts and associations or power groups.

"...It's obviously a business and they [ABC] need the Los Angeles—Dallas game to be a big game, to fight the excellent movies on Sunday night TV. It's obvious, it's blatant. In my opinion, it's a disservice to the public."

How could the 49ers fight that? Simply by playing well, Walsh suggested, and so they would, for a much longer time than anybody thought possible.

5

NO. 4, AND COUNTING

The problem with success in the NFL is that there's little time to savor it. The 49ers could be proud of their win over Dallas, but they still had a light workout on Monday, a heavy workout on Wednesday, a trip to Milwaukee on Friday, and a game against the Green Bay Packers on Sunday. The Packers hadn't been a championship team since Vince Lombardi had retired, but that made little difference: they were still capable of winning on that well-known "any given Sunday." A loss to the Packers would wipe out the win over Dallas; it would be like a tennis player breaking his opponent's service and then losing his own.

The 49ers were aware of that. Right guard Randy Cross started thinking about it only a few hours after the Dallas game, amidst congratulations from fans as he was trying to eat dinner in a Peninsula restaurant. The fans were ecstatically telling him, "You're going to the Super Bowl," but Cross wasn't buying. Not yet, anyway.

"It's great to be excited," he said, "but you've got to be realistic about it. As good as we've looked at times in the last two weeks, it doesn't take a genius to remember how good we didn't look against New Orleans, three games ago, so we're not exactly incapable of our own little miscues."

The 49ers knew from recent and painful experience how easy it was to let down. Just a year ago they had upset New England and then came out thinking of where they were going to spend Christmas the next week against New Orleans. The Saints, who had lost 13 in a row, stormed to a 35-7 halftime lead before the 49ers recovered to mount that spectacular comeback for a 38-35 overtime win.

Against the Packers the year before, the 49ers had squandered a 13-0 lead and lost 23-16. The Niners wouldn't be overconfident this Sunday, and Cross was optimistic because he liked the spirit of the team.

"We have *real* enthusiasm," he said. "Not just guys jumping up and down. You felt like giving them all pom-poms. We've got guys who have something to be enthusiastic about."

It was a little difficult to maintain that enthusiasm when the 49ers played the Packers in Milwaukee that gray and nasty Sunday. Rain started falling in the first quarter, making the grass turf slick, and winds gusting up to 40 mph made any pass longer than 15 yards a real adventure.

But the 49ers, meeting a new test every week, showed that they were capable of beating a mediocre team on a bad day, one of the important attributes of a good team.

Bill Walsh would term this a tactical win for the 49ers. Because the defense was playing so well and because weather conditions were terrible, he called a conservative game—so the offense wouldn't give the Packers a chance at an easy score. (Walsh calls all the plays, though quarterback Joe Montana has the right to change them at the line of scrimmage.)

The 49er offense produced just enough at the right times. Their first score came right before the end of the first half when, trailing 3-0, the 49ers marched 71 yards before settling for a Ray Wersching field goal.

In the third quarter, the 49ers had the wind at their backs; they knew they had to score in that quarter because the Packers would have the wind advantage in the fourth quarter. Johnny Davis climaxed a long drive with a short touchdown, from only inches out.

The third high point for the offense came in the last quarter, when they used up over seven minutes with a drive that finally ended with another field goal. In that fourth quarter, the 49ers had the ball more than twelve-and-a-half minutes, effectively negating the Packers' wind advantage.

Quarterback coach Sam Wyche said Montana, who completed 23 of 32 passes, had played his smartest game yet as a 49er, calling audibles to adjust formations and counter the Packers' defensive tactics. "A lot of little things that we've been stressing all year are starting to pay off for us now," said Wyche.

But this was primarily a defensive win for the 49ers. Defensive coordinator Chuck Studley, as imaginative on his side of the scrimmage line as Walsh is on the offensive side, came up with a new defense, using the 3-4 but putting Fred Dean in as a weakside linebacker alongside Dwaine Board. The idea was to have both Dean and Board, the 49ers quickest linemen, rushing from the same side to pressure Green Bay quarterback Lynn Dickey.

The Packers countered by using four wide receivers and double-teaming Dean, but that only left room for Lawrence Pillers to rush from the other side. Pillers sacked Dickey three times and twice nailed running back Harlen Huckleby for losses on running plays.

When it was all over, the 49ers had won their fourth straight, the longest winning streak since 1976, and were a game ahead of Los Angeles in the NFC Western Division—and the Rams were coming to town.

6

THE PERILS OF PAULINE

San Franciscans like to think of the 49ers-Rams series as a great rivalry, yet, historically at least, that's stretching a point. "Rivalry" implies that either team could win, but somebody had forgotten to tell the 49ers.

The 49ers hadn't beaten the Rams in San Francisco since 1966; their last win in Los Angeles had been in 1976 when they pitched a 16-0 shutout. Only four players remained from that 49er team: Keith Fahnhorst, Randy Cross, John Ayers, and Willie Harper.

Even when Dick Nolan's teams had won three straight divisional titles in the early seventies, they had beaten the Rams only once in six games. Overall, the Rams-49ers series stood at 41-19-2. Some rivalry.

But this time, the Rams looked ready to be taken. They were struggling a bit at 4-3. Injuries had hurt them, particularly in the offensive line; the Rams' strength always had been in their ability to control the line of scrimmage, and they could no longer do that. Quarterback Pat Haden had problems throwing long, and, at 5-feet-10, in seeing over the heads of defensive linemen who sometimes loomed nearly a foot taller.

Other deeper and off-field problems bedeviled the Rams. Georgia Frontiere, who had inherited the club when Carroll Rosenbloom died, was setting the women's movement back 50 years with her inept interference in what had been a model NFL operation. Her meddling had caused ace personnel director Dick

Steinberg, who had selected many of the Rams' top players in the draft, to move on.

She had stripped much of the authority from Rams' general manager Don Klosterman, who now had to get final approval on everything from Frontiere. Her stranglehold on the purse strings had been a primary factor in the loss of Vince Ferragamo, on the verge of becoming the best quarterback in the NFL, to Canada.

On top of all that, the Rams had had problems with their veteran players ever since rookie defensive back Johnnie Johnson had been signed to a huge bonus and salary in 1980; that seeming over-compensation had been a factor in the departure of Jack Reynolds.

A bizarre episode earlier in the year, when the club had tried to cut defensive end Fred Dryer, was also causing repercussions. Sometimes a star player negotiates a "no-cut" contract, which simply means he still gets paid even if dropped from the team. Dryer's contract went further: it specified that he couldn't be dropped from the team without his permission. When the Rams first tried to cut Dryer, he calmly reminded them of that clause. So they kept him around for a time, but doing nothing. Finally they cut him again; Dryer sued and joined CBS as a color commentator. Great for team harmony.

Forty-Niner fans sensed the kill, and their sizzling young team was a slight favorite. It was the hottest ticket in town; fans who had had no trouble getting tickets for the A's-Yankees' American League baseball playoff earlier in the month learned to their dismay that they'd have to watch the 49ers and Rams on television.

An added factor for this game, and one that became more and more important as the season went on, was the field. A two-day Rolling Stones concert at Candlestick preceded the game, and the turf had been badly torn up. The Candlestick field, never a good one, had become probably the worst natural-grass field in the league.

For the rest of the year, no runner would gain as much as 100 yards in a game at Candlestick. At all the remaining home games, members of the hard-working maintenance crew—the "Sod Squad"—would race out at every timeout and hurriedly replace the divots, some of them a foot long.

Everybody seemed to be running in slow motion on the field. Problems were especially noticeable at the south end, the infield during baseball season. Runners who tried to make sharp cuts there found their feet flying out from under them. Field goal kickers often as not fell down on their follow-throughs.

But, though this bothered the players, it didn't faze the spectators. No one who got a ticket to this game regretted it. The game wasn't one of spectacular plays, but it was excruciatingly exciting and a real test for weak hearts.

The 49ers got off almost as fast as they had in the win over Dallas, scoring twice in the first period on Joe Montana passes, the first a 14-yarder to Fred Solomon, the second a 41-yard strike to Dwight Clark. But this wasn't to be the lopsided contest the Dallas game had been.

The Rams came back in the second quarter as Frank Corral kicked a 25-yard field goal (his only successful field goal attempt in five tries during the day) and Mike Guman scored on a two-yard plunge to cut the Niners' lead to 14-10.

The 49ers retaliated with a 42-yard field goal by Ray Wersching, set up by a thrilling 50-yard strike from Montana to Earl Cooper just before halftime. Then Wersching did it again, this time from the 18, to make it 20-10 in the third quarter.

About that time a huge roar went up from the stands: it had just been announced that the New York Giants had beaten Atlanta, 27-24, knocking the Falcons back to a 4-4 record. Playoff talk had been downplayed by Bill Walsh and the Niners, but the fans knew what Atlanta's loss meant, and so did the players.

"We saw that score and we knew we couldn't let up," said Fahnhorst.

They didn't, although they had to survive a fourth quarter of incredible tension to win the game.

The Rams closed the gap to 20-17 with a touchdown late in the third quarter coming on a 16-yard pass from Haden to running back Wendell Tyler.

That set the stage for a nerve-racking test of the 49ers' courage. Many key games and events were part of their march to the Super Bowl, but in the fourth quarter of this game the 49ers proved beyond doubt that they belonged in the NFL's elite.

Five times in a row the 49er offense was unable to get a first down and had to punt. Five times in a row the Rams got the ball in good field position, three of those times inside San Francisco territory.

It was like the "Perils of Pauline." Each time the Rams got the ball, it seemed this would be the time when that Los Angeles locomotive would finally run over the 49ers. But each time, some Niner would come up with a big play to frustrate the Rams once again.

That somebody, oftener than not, was Fred Dean. More

and more, Dean's value to the club was becoming obvious. "He's one of those players like Ted Hendricks and Ronnie Lott who just have the ability to make the big play," said Walsh.

It's probably a matter of personality as much as physical ability. There are players who love the spotlight, and they get it by making the big play when the game or championship is on the line. Reggie Jackson hits home runs in the World Series; Hendricks blocks a field goal to win a game. And Dean makes the key quarterback sacks. "I feel I can get to the quarterback anytime I really have to," he says, and his play often supports that contention.

When the 49ers traded for Dean, Walsh noted that his chief value would be in protecting a lead in the fourth quarter, and there is no better example of that than what Dean did to the Rams in the fourth quarter of that October game:

—On third-and-five from the San Francisco 37 on the Rams' first possession, Fred Dean and Jim Stuckey combined to sack Pat Haden and force a punt.

—On third-and-five from the San Francisco 46 on the Rams' next possession, Dean's pressure forced Haden to the other side, where he was sacked by Lawrence Pillers.

—With just under three minutes remaining and the Rams at third-and-ten on the San Francisco 34, Dean sacked Haden again, forcing another punt.

—On the Rams' last drive Dean sacked Haden twice, for eight- and eleven-yard losses. A determined Haden kept the drive going with desperation passes until the Rams came up against a third-and-ten on the San Francisco 31, with 46 seconds left. Perhaps fearing Dean's rush, Haden called a draw play. Guman was stopped after four yards by...Fred Dean.

That forced Corral to try another field goal. For the fourth straight time Corral missed, sealing the 49er victory. Corral, who had kicked 10 of 12 before that game, blamed his performance on "the worst field I've ever seen." He was probably right about the field, but Wersching was kicking on the same field.

Dean's sacks were obvious, but less obviously, his mere presence in a 49er uniform forced the Rams to change their style and their game plan. Early on, for instance, they often threw on first down because Dean *wouldn't* be in the game. In passing situations, the Rams often ran, trying to counteract his effectiveness.

They even tried double-teaming Dean, which only opened up avenues for other 49er linemen. Doug France tried to arm-wrestle him, and on one play, Dean was literally tackled. But in the end, nothing worked when Dean really wanted to move on the quarterback.

There were other stars for the 49ers. Montana tied his career high with 287 yards passing and extended to 99 his club record for passes without interception.

But it was really a defensive victory, even though the 49ers yielded 401 yards, because they would not break in that critical fourth quarter.

"The good thing is that we're winning now and we're not playing that super, wide-open, blast 'em off offense," said quarterback coach Sam Wyche. "The defense is playing super."

The 49ers were obviously on a roll. They had won five straight and their 6-2 record was surpassed in the NFL only by Philadelphia's 7-1. More importantly, they had a two-game lead in their division over the Rams and Falcons, both at 4-4, and nobody else had that big a margin.

What meant the most, at least to the four players who had been on the team in 1976, was that the victory had come over the Rams.

"Dallas doesn't even compare to this," said Fahnhorst. "It's unbelievable. I'm not going to come down for five days. It's been a long, frustrating time for us."

Cross agreed. "This is a lot of satisfaction after all the knocks and all the bullshit we had to take for the last five years. It's just like a little bit of vindication. We've beaten two quote, unquote TEAMS. Now, we can't be criticized for just beating the little guys. That's a nice feeling."

And there were more of those nice feelings to come.

7

45 AGAINST 50,000

Football as coached by Bill Walsh is an intellectual exercise, but it's also a physical game—and that was the essence of the problem for the 49ers as they journeyed to Pittsburgh in the ninth week of the season, with their five-game winning streak on the line.

The Steelers, though not the team that had dominated the NFL in the seventies, still were a very punishing bunch, an apt reflection of the working-class city they represented. Highly skilled players like quarterback Terry Bradshaw and wide receiver Lynn Swann might dominate the headlines, but the real key to the Steelers' success was physical intimidation.

Normally coaches look only at game films from the current season, trying to pick up tendencies and note strengths and weaknesses of the team they are about to play. This week, though, Walsh looked at films of the Oakland Raiders' win over Pittsburgh the year before. He wanted to see how the Raiders had done it.

He wasn't looking for specific plays; the 49ers actually used only one play, a run that worked twice for five yards each time, that the Raiders had used. What Walsh was concerned about was style, and he learned that the Raiders beat the Steelers by hitting as hard as they were hit, disdaining fancy tactics.

Walsh decided the 49ers would have to do the same. "The coaches told us at the beginning of the week, 'We're going after them'," said right guard Randy Cross later. This would be no chess game.

Walsh also had to counter some psychological problems, one of them being simply that the 49ers were due for a letdown after five straight wins, especially coming off such an emotional victory as the one over the Rams. Psychologists claim a person who hits an extreme emotional peak cannot again reach such heights for eight days, making it a bit difficult for NFL teams playing games seven days apart.

For this confrontation, Walsh dealt with that problem by giving his players more work, including looking at extra game films of the Steelers. "They didn't complain," he said. "They wanted to look at extra films. Some even took films home."

The other problem was the fact that the 49ers were playing in Pittsburgh's Three Rivers Stadium, possibly the most hostile setting for a visiting team in the entire league. The Steelers played their best at home, particularly against National Conference teams. They were 15-2 at home against NFC teams since the merger of the NFL and AFL in 1970, and hadn't lost at Three Rivers against an NFC team since 1971.

Walsh used his historical knowledge to prepare his players for what they would face at Three Rivers. On Wednesday, two days before the team left for Pittsburgh, he recounted the lesson British troops had learned in Burma during World War II.

The British troops, he told his players, were retreating before the Japanese advance. Periodically, the Japanese would capture a few of the British troops and kill them. Finally, the number of troops down to perhaps a thousand, the British found themselves backed up against a mountain. They had no choice but to fight back.

The 49ers, Walsh said, were backed up against that mountain, and the Steelers were only part of the problem. "We're 45 against 50,000 [fans]," he told his team. "We have to fight back."

A bit melodramatic, to be sure, but the 49ers took it to heart. From the start that Sunday, they played as if they were fighting a war, and one they intended to win. They slugged it out with the Steelers, never giving an inch.

Strong safety Carlton Williamson was the chief warrior. In the second quarter, Steeler wide receiver Calvin Sweeney caught a pass in front of Williamson, and Williamson smashed him to the turf, a legal but very hard hit. Sweeney lay there for some time before getting up.

On the Steelers' next possession, Williamson blasted

another Pittsburgh wide receiver, John Stallworth, and again, it was some time before Stallworth got up.

Ironically, the scouting report on Williamson as a college senior was that he wasn't much of a hitter. The 49ers hadn't believed that then and they certainly didn't believe it now. Neither did the Steelers. Receivers had already learned to brace themselves for brutal tackles by Ronnie Lott; now they had to be just as aware of what would happen when they caught a pass in Williamson's territory. A receiver who's thinking of how hard he's about to be hit has a difficult time concentrating on the pass being thrown his way.

The 49ers were so aggressive that fights broke out early in the game. Walsh didn't apologize for that.

"We had to be physical to survive," he said. "The fights were not ragged, cheap shots. They were hard-hitting plays where we would not back off, and neither would they. That's a good sign.

"The fights showed up early. I interpret that as positive. It means we played head-to-head from the start and didn't resort to fighting when we were behind. The fights were more important in the early part than scoring. We established ourselves on the field."

The 49ers also established themselves on the scoreboard, breaking a scoreless tie with ten quick points just before the half.

The first score was set up by an Eric Wright interception, which gave the 49ers the ball on the Pittsburgh 46. Seven plays later, the 49ers were in the end zone.

The touchdown came on a five-yard pass from Joe Montana to Charle Young, but the key play was a 23-yard pass from Montana to Dwight Clark earlier on the drive. Clark admitted later that he had had his own kind of problem preparing for the game. "When I was in high school, these guys were my heroes—Bradshaw, Stallworth, and Swann. I was trying to get that out of my mind and not let them intimidate me. But after I got out there on the field, I saw that we're as good as those guys."

Ray Wersching added the PAT to make it 7-0, and he hardly had a chance to catch his breath before he was back in action. Williamson recovered a Frank Pollard fumble on the Pittsburgh 37. Two plays later, Montana scrambled eight yards to the 28, and then Wersching kicked a 45-yard field goal with just three seconds left on the clock.

The Pittsburgh fans were booing their heroes as they left

the field at halftime, down 10-zip, but those boos rapidly changed to cheers as the second half began.

Montana had extended his club record of passes without interception to 122 when the streak was broken in shocking fashion: Mel Blount intercepted on the sidelines and scrambled 50 yards for a touchdown, with just 4:24 elapsed in the third quarter.

Less than four minutes later Montana threw another interception, this one to Pittsburgh middle linebacker Jack Lambert, who returned it 31 yards to the San Francisco 22. Bradshaw threw a touchdown pass to Jim Smith on the next play.

There was a reason for Montana's suddenly erratic play: he had injured his ribs badly the week before against the Rams, and the ribs both pained him and restricted his throwing.

Montana's ribs had not bothered him during the week, but warming up before the game and thinking about playing before friends and relatives from nearby, he started hyperventilating and his ribs started to hurt again. So much for Joe Cool. Montana, reluctantly had worn a flak vest to protect his ribs. "I hate to wear it," he said. "It's like saying, 'Here's a target; aim for it.' "

After the kickoff following the second Pittsburgh touchdown, the 49ers were set to start from their 11. If Walsh had thought his team was backed up against a mountain before the game, how about now? They were down four points, the Pittsburgh crowd was going crazy, the Niners' quarterback was hurt, and they were deep in their own territory.

So all San Francisco did was drive 69 yards. Though their field goal attempt was blocked, that was less important than that the 49ers had shown the Steelers they couldn't, wouldn't be intimidated.

With only 10:46 left in the game, the 49ers got the break they needed: Williamson intercepted and returned the ball 28 yards to the Pittsburgh 43. From there, the 49ers simply hammered in for the winning touchdown. The key gainer was a 23-yard Montana-to-Solomon pass; Walt Easley went in from two yards out, and the Niners were up, 17-14.

(Easley, who went to West Virginia University, 75 miles from Pittsburgh, was one of three key 49ers who had once played ball close to Three Rivers Stadium: Montana is from Monongahela, a small town in southwest Pennsylvania, and Williamson played college ball at the University of Pittsburgh.)

The 49ers didn't have the game clinched yet, not with five minutes remaining and the Steelers with the ball. Pittsburgh mounted one last drive, using up three minutes to get to the San Francisco 34, where they had third down and one yard to go.

Probably the most curious play of the game followed. It seemed almost certain the Steelers would run the ball. If they failed to get the short yardage on third down, they would still have another down to try. The Pittsburgh offensive line is often considered the best in the league, and it was inconceivable that they couldn't make enough room for a Steeler back to get one yard in two tries.

But Bradshaw thought he saw something in the 49er secondary. Changing his call at the line of scrimmage [and almost getting a delay-of-game penalty in doing so], he faked the run and dropped back to pass.

Bradshaw wanted to hit running back Frank Pollard coming out of the backfield. Pollard was the responsibility of free safety Dwight Hicks, who was lined up as a linebacker in the short-yardage defense.

But as Bradshaw set to pass, Hicks saw a crack in the offensive line. With the gut instinct and quick reactions of a great athlete, he took off. "There was nobody there to block me, and I knew Bradshaw would have to do something quick when I got there."

What Bradshaw had to do was dump the ball off to tight end Randy Grossman to escape a sack; Grossman was tackled by 49er corner Eric Wright for a two-yard loss. The Steelers went from two chances to make a yard to one desperation chance to make three long yards.

This time, the Steelers really did have to pass, and the 49ers came with their best rush of the day, forcing Bradshaw to throw an incomplete pass. The 49ers had their sixth straight win, 17-14, and one of their most satisfying.

It was fitting that a defensive back made the big play at the end because it was the secondary which dominated the game, even though the 49ers couldn't put on much of a pass rush against the great Steeler offensive line.

"Their secondary is the best I've seen all year," said Bradshaw. "I'm the one who looked like the rookie, not them."

Hicks, Williamson, and Wright all had interceptions, and Williamson, Wright, and Lott also recovered Pittsburgh fumbles.

"Our young defensive backs could very well be the best in football," said Walsh. "I don't think there's ever been a rookie backfield that played like this one in the history of the game."

The 49er numbers were mounting. Their six straight wins was the team's longest streak in a season. At 7-2 they shared the league's best record with Philadelphia and led NFC West by two games. Within a four-week stretch they had beaten three of the teams that had been among the most dominant in the NFL for a decade: Dallas, Los Angeles, and Pittsburgh.

Not bad for a team that wasn't good enough to be on Monday Night Football.

8

NO PRESTON RILEY THIS TIME

Around the league, people thought...well, they really didn't know what to think of the 49ers. Judged by conventional standards, the whole thing didn't make any sense. Who are these people, and why are they winning?

And *how* are they winning: field goal wins over Pittsburgh and Los Angeles, only a touchdown over New Orleans, just ten points over Green Bay? Were they really good or just lucky?

Bill Walsh thought he knew why the wins came so hard. "We don't have a dominant runner," he explained. "The teams that can control games are those teams with the runners who get 1200-1500 yards in a season. We don't have that kind of runner, so that's why you're seeing these 17-14, 20-17 games."

To the rest of the league, the 49ers seemed to consist largely of players nobody else wanted; there were, in fact 15 free agents on the roster. They had a quarterback who supposedly couldn't throw long, a wide receiver who had been a tenth-round draft pick because he had little speed, an offensive tackle who should be playing guard, and three rookies playing in the defensive backfield. Nobody had ever heard of such a thing.

Those who looked a little closer saw that the San Francisco 49ers were not a team that could be judged by conventional standards. For one thing, Walsh had an extraordinary ability to turn a debit into an asset.

There was, for instance, the case of the guard playing tackle, Dan Audick. Walsh's original plan had been to start Ken

Bungarda, a giant of a man who was being switched from
defense to offense. Ron Singleton, the starter at left tackle the
year before and the one weak spot in the line, had been released.

Bungarda, injured in the pre-season, was out for the
season, so Walsh traded a draft pick to San Diego to get Audick,
a reserve for the Chargers, who were deep in offensive
linemen. (It was, incidentally, the first of three trades between the
two clubs; the 49ers later got running back Amos Lawrence and,
of course, Fred Dean. Because the teams are in different
conferences and thus not directly competitive, the Chargers
didn't worry that the trades might strengthen the 49ers, which
they did.)

Audick is a fine lineman, but he lacks the size of the
typical offensive tackle. Walsh predicated much of his quick-pass
offense on the knowledge that Audick could not be expected to
consistently hold out defensive ends long enough for long passes.

But, at the same time, Audick is faster than most tackles,
so Walsh devised plays which called for Audick to pull out and
lead the blocking on a run, usually the responsibility of a guard.
That thoroughly confused defenses.

Another example of San Francisco's unconventionality:
their running backs. Paul Hofer was the only 49er back who
could do it all—run inside or out, block, catch passes. But Hofer's
knee limited him to spot appearances and he was seldom an
important factor.

The other backs were all essentially one-dimensional:
Johnny Davis and Walt Easley could run up the middle; Ricky
Patton was more of an outside runner; Earl Cooper was being
used almost entirely as a pass receiver out of the backfield.

It's certainly a lot easier to gear an offense around a
Tony Dorsett or Earl Campbell type of runner. But it's also
easier for a defense to prepare for that kind of offense. With the
49ers, other teams never knew quite what to expect from the San
Francisco running attack. A different back would be the key
every week.

And that's exactly what it was for the rest of the 49ers,
too. It was a *team*, not overly dependent on any one individual,
with the exception of Joe Montana.

Every week, Walsh would tell his team, "Somebody in this
room is going to win this game for us."

And each week it *was* somebody different. Against
Atlanta, in the tenth week, it was two men, safety Dwight Hicks
and tight end Charle Young, who were the key players, and each
had an interesting story.

Hicks was one of the 49er free agents, a fact which always astounded Walsh. "I don't see how anybody could watch Dwight Hicks play and not think that he was going to be an outstanding player," said the coach.

But somebody had made a mistake on Hicks. Twice.

Hicks was drafted in 1978 by the Detroit Lions and survived until the next-to-last cut in training camp that summer. He then went to the Canadian League and played out the season.

The next summer he signed with the Philadelphia Eagles and made it until the last cut of that training camp. Discouraged, he went home to Southfield, Michigan (a suburb of Detroit), and managed a health foods store. He thought he was through with football.

But Walsh was desperate for secondary help that first season, and he called Hicks to give him a tryout. It didn't bother Walsh that Hicks had been cut by two teams; quite the contrary, in fact. "Sometimes," he says, "players who aren't quite ready will go through a couple of training camps and become much better players. The experience of playing against proven players is far better than anything they get in college ball."

Hicks was an immediate standout with the 49ers. The first year, playing in only eight games, he led the team in interceptions with five. The next year, in a full 16-game season, he intercepted four passes and was involved in 92 tackles, 54 of them unassisted.

Young, too, was a castoff, though of a different kind. He had started his pro career in spectacular fashion, catching 167 passes in his first three years with the Philadelphia Eagles and being named Rookie of the Year in 1973 and All-Pro in 1974 and 1975. He seemed the prototype tight end, with both speed and size.

But after his fourth year the Eagles traded him to Los Angeles. Nobody could figure why the Rams traded for him; once they got him, they almost never used him. He caught only 36 passes in three years while playing behind Terry Nelson, a tight end who would be flattered to be called mediocre. Before the 1980 season, the 49ers got Young from the Rams for a 1983 draft choice.

Young, an ordained minister active in youth work, is philosophical about his three semi-idle years. "I learned patience, to persevere, to cope and deal with problems. When a man can deal with the situation I was in with the Rams, it tells something about that man's character. Besides, playing so little for them probably added three years to my career."

No longer possessing the speed that made him a great deep threat early in his career, Young nevertheless became a valuable clutch receiver for the 49ers, and his teammates recognized his leadership qualities by voting him the Len Eshmont award in 1981 as the most inspirational player.

The 49ers would need everything they could get from Hicks and Young, and all the others, to beat the Falcons. Atlanta had been the last team to beat the 49ers, and the Falcons were still only two games back; a win would bring them within one game of the 49ers, and many observers thought that might be the beginning of the end for the Niners.

Once again the 49ers got off to a fast start, taking a 10-0 lead into the dressing room at halftime after Montana threw a 14-yard touchdown pass to Fred Solomon and Ray Wersching kicked a 48-yard field goal.

The Falcons cut it to 10-7 in the third quarter as Steve Bartkowski drove them 75 yards to a score. At that point, the 49ers seemed in trouble, even though leading; their offense had sputtered and the Falcons had moved so easily on their last drive that it was obvious they would score at least one more touchdown.

But the 49ers had been an opportunistic team, seemingly able to make the big play or drive when they most needed it, and they displayed that ability once again, quickly driving 76 yards in 13 plays.

They used everything in the drive, including reverses by both Solomon and Dwight Clark and a run-pass option by Ricky Patton, who chose to run.

On third down from the Atlanta three, Montana lobbed a pass high to the back of the end zone, giving Young a chance to leap high above the smaller Atlanta defensive backs to make the catch...which he did.

"We had three plays like that in the game plan," Montana said. "They call it a 'drift.' I ran to the right, and Charle runs along the end line from the right to the left and then back to the right."

At 17-7, the 49ers felt pretty confident, even though Ronnie Lott was thrown out of the game with 5:39 left when he slugged Atlanta receiver Alfred Jackson while San Francisco's Saladin Martin was returning his first NFL interception.

"I don't even know what happened," said Lott. Television replays clearly showed him hitting Jackson, and teammates thought he might have hit Jackson more than once, but it's entirely possible that Lott didn't know he had done it.

Lott undergoes an amazing transformation when he puts on a uniform. Away from football he is mild-mannered and soft-spoken, but he's a tiger on the field. Many players experience somewhat similar changes, but Lott's is extreme. It's almost as if he's playing in a hypnotic trance. That concentration is one reason he is a superior player, of course.

With just 2:23 left, the 49ers still held that 17-7 lead and seemed to be in control. That feeling didn't last long. Bartkowski, thought by some to be the best quarterback in the game, engineered a classic drive, taking the Falcons 76 yards to a touchdown in just six plays. More remarkably, taking just one timeout (plus the timeout at the two-minute warning), he used only 40 seconds on the clock. He passed 25 yards to Jackson for the touchdown, and Mick Luckhurst added the PAT to make it 17-14.

Everybody in the park knew what was coming next: an onside kick. It did—three times. The first two were nullified by penalties, one against each team. Luckhurst, a former soccer player who can kick with more precision than a kicker who's never known any sport but football, lofted another one down the west sideline. It was fumbled by the 49ers and recovered by the Falcons.

Shades of Preston Riley! Forty-Niner fans who could remember 1972 were convinced that the Falcons would sweep down the field and score, and that almost happened.

The Falcons advanced to the San Francisco 17, where they had first-and-ten with still 1:23 remaining, plenty of time for Bartkowski to work on the 49er secondary, crippled by the loss of Lott, their best defender.

It was the time coaches call "gut checks," when the butterflies start fluttering in the stomachs because the game is up for grabs. The 49ers of previous years had lost games just like this one, but not this team, not this year. The Los Angeles game, when the 49ers stopped those five fourth-quarter drives, had given the young 49ers the equivalent of a season's experience under great pressure. Nothing fazed them anymore.

Bartkowski went back to pass. He thought he had Junior Miller open, but Hicks came over from the middle, where he had been helping double-cover Jenkins, to make a game-saving interception at the three-yard line.

"I got a good look at Bartkowski, and he was following the primary receiver [Miller] all the way," said Hicks. "Because of the pass rush, he didn't have time to look anywhere else."

That last comment by Hicks was a telling one: once again the 49er defense was controlling the flow of the game, forcing the other team to do something it didn't want to do.

That had been true throughout the Atlanta game, in marked contrast to the first time the teams had met. In the first game, the Falcons controlled the ball with their excellent running attack and exploited the 49er defense with long passes.

In this game, though, the 49ers neutralized the Atlanta runners, who gained only 74 yards and averaged just 2.9 a carry, and their pass rush kept Bartkowski from throwing long. He was pressured so much that he started to go to quick, slant-in passes. They were effective at times, but that wasn't what he wanted to throw. Any time you can force a team to change from what it does best, you've taken a big step toward victory.

For the first time, 49er players started talking about the playoffs; Young even said they were concerned not just about making the playoffs but about getting a record good enough to play at home.

Their confidence was understandable. The win over the Falcons had pushed the San Francisco record to 8-2. Meanwhile, the Falcons and Rams, who lost to New Orleans, were three games back at 5-5. And the win had stretched the 49er streak to seven games.

When would it all end?

9

THE STREAK ENDS

Next week, to the Cleveland Browns on a gloomy, early winter day at Candlestick.

Perhaps it was a consolation to the 49ers that relatively few people saw this game. A violent storm had hit on Thursday of that week, drenching the Bay Area with near-record rainfall, and more of the same had been predicted for Sunday. As it turned out, though the skies threatened to loose buckets at any moment, just a few drops fell during the game. Only 52,455 fans defied the weather forecaster to come to Candlestick, the smallest crowd since the second home game, against New Orleans.

Nor was the game televised locally, an irony because former 49er quarterback John Brodie was working his first game involving the 49ers in his eight-year broadcasting career with NBC.

Brodie talks frequently with 49er coach Bill Walsh, and sometimes even drops by the team's Redwood City offices to look at game films. He has nothing but praise for Walsh and his organizational skills: "He knows exactly what he wants and how to go about getting it."

As a former quarterback, Brodie especially liked Joe Montana, for many of the same reasons that Walsh did. He thought observers who criticized Montana because he couldn't throw the ball from one end of the field to the other were missing the point.

"It isn't only the spiral a passer puts on the ball, or the

length he can throw it, or how he scrambles out of the pocket, or even the way he reads defenses," said Brodie.

"It's all those things, yes, but it's that other thing, the intangible. It's a feeling of command, maybe even a little arrogance. Montana has it."

Brodie was partial, because he had pushed Walsh to draft Montana in the first place—not that Walsh needed much of a push.

"I saw Joe Montana a couple of times with Notre Dame and clearly he was quality stuff," said Brodie. "Then at the CBS Hall of Fame dinner, I sat next to Montana. We chatted for perhaps 40 minutes and I was impressed by his attitude.

"I really wanted Montana to be a 49er and I talked with Bill Walsh before the 1979 draft. I wasn't telling him anything—he wanted Montana, too—and I think his enthusiasm increased as we spoke of Montana's cool. Bill thought Montana would be available in the second round."

Before the draft, Walsh went to the Los Angeles area (Montana had moved there two months before the draft) and worked Montana with UCLA running back James Owens. Walsh was impressed with them and wanted to draft both. What he knew (and Brodie didn't) was that he would draft Owens first.

When Owens was taken on the second round by the 49ers, Brodie made a quick phone call to the team offices to find out why Walsh hadn't taken Montana. Walsh admitted he was gambling that other teams hadn't rated Montana so highly. "I think we can get him on the third round," he told Brodie.

As he is so frequently, Walsh was right. On the first round, Cincinnati had taken Jack Thompson and the New York Giants had drafted Phil Simms. Walsh liked Thompson but had known he would have no chance to get him, because the 49ers had no first-round pick (gone in the O.J. Simpson trade). He also liked Simms, and he might have been tempted to go for him had Simms slipped through to the second round.

Another quarterback, Steve Fuller, was taken by Kansas City on the second round, but Walsh had no interest in Fuller. He had gone to Clemson to watch Fuller work out and wasn't impressed, but the trip hadn't been wasted. On the tenth round that year, he drafted the receiver Fuller had thrown to in that workout, Dwight Clark.

Nobody was interested enough in Montana to draft him, even though he lasted almost all the way through the third round. The 49ers had traded their own pick on that round but had gotten Dallas's third-round pick in another trade. That meant they had to wait until Dallas's turn came up in the round, just two from the end, but Montana was still available.

"All it took was seeing him in a mini-camp to realize he was going to be something special," said Brodie.

Montana wasn't something special on this day against Cleveland and neither were his teammates. The 49ers were emotionally spent, and it showed in their error-filled play.

Their problem was understandable. There is only so much the human psyche can take. The 49ers had won a club record seven in a row (the 1948 team won ten straight, but that was in the All-America Conference, and the NFL doesn't recognize AAC statistics), and most of them had been big games. In the last five weeks, they had beaten Dallas, Los Angeles, Pittsburgh, and Atlanta, and Los Angeles was coming up the next week.

The offense was especially flat, unable to score a touchdown for the first time since Walsh had been 49er coach. Five times in the first three quarters, the 49ers drove within the Cleveland 25-yard line and each time had to settle for a Ray Wersching field goal, coincidentally every one from 28 yards.

A sixth opportunity came with a Dwight Hicks interception that put the ball on the Cleveland 31; that chance was wasted when Montana threw three incomplete passes.

Everything seemed to go wrong for the 49ers. Montana was penalized for intentionally grounding when he threw the ball away to prevent being tackled in the end zone; the penalty gave the Browns a two-point safety, the same result that a sack would have brought. A Walt Easley run to the Cleveland two, which would probably have set up a 49er touchdown, was nullified by a 15-yard penalty when Easley slugged Cleveland cornerback Ron Bolton after his run. Fred Dean bruised his sternum and missed most of the fourth quarter.

With all that, the 49ers still had a 12-5 lead at the beginning of the fourth quarter and were in position to put the game out of reach of the struggling Browns when Niner Bill Ring recovered a fumbled punt by Dino Hall on the Cleveland 21. Even a San Francisco field goal might be enough, and a touchdown would certainly seal the victory.

On the first play, though, Montana threw to Clark, who fell on the slippery Candlestick turf. The pass was tipped by rookie corner Hanford Dixon and intercepted by Browns linebacker Dick Ambrose. That was the last opportunity the 49ers had to score.

In the broadcast booth, Brodie was telling his listeners, "Joe tried to make a great play out of a bad situation. He threw off balance. He doesn't do that too often. If he never did it, we'd all be bowing down to him."

Soon Hall redeemed himself by returning a punt 40 yards, and the game was about to turn around. With Dean, their best pass rusher, out of the game, the 49ers stayed in a 3-4 defense. Walsh had said the 49ers hoped to pressure Cleveland quarterback Brian Sipe with blitzes, but the tactic didn't work. Sipe eventually passed to Reggie Rucker for 21 yards and the touchdown that enabled the Browns to tie the game.

Rucker, a 12-year veteran, fooled 49er corner Eric Wright because he acted as if the pass weren't coming to him, waiting until the last second to put up his hands to catch it. "That's one of the finest plays by a wide receiver I've seen in some time," Brodie said. "He turned Wright around, and Wright couldn't react because he didn't know the ball was there."

The Browns had one drive left, and again, the 49ers felt the absence of Dean. The key play was a 38-yard pass from Sipe to Rucker on the first-and-twenty, a situation in which the 49ers normally use a 4-3 defense, including Dean. Without him, they were in a 3-4 and couldn't effectively pressure Sipe.

With 43 seconds left Matt Bahr kicked a 24-yard field goal, giving Cleveland the 15-12 win and ending the 49ers' streak. Ironically, Bahr had played for the 49ers earlier in the season, while Wersching was out with a pulled muscle. When Wersching returned, Walsh traded Bahr because he felt Wersching was the more reliable kicker. "Ray has just made so many pressure kicks for us," said Walsh.

It's a reasonable assumption that if Dean had not been injured, the 49ers would have won the game. In the first three quarters Cleveland passed for 72 yards; on the fourth-period drives, when Dean was out, Sipe passed for 93.

Still, Walsh was more concerned with his team's offensive failures. "Our failure to score is very obviously what cost us," he said. "We finally ran into a situation where we put too much pressure on our own defense. When one single touchdown beats you, obviously you have to improve."

But though the 49ers lost, they stayed three games ahead in the NFC West because both Atlanta and Los Angeles lost. Now, with only five games left, the 49ers had a chance to bury the Rams by winning in Anaheim the next Sunday. They'd be ready.

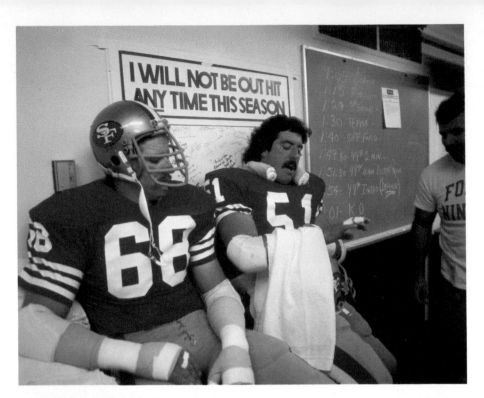

(Overleaf) Bill Walsh listens to assistants calling from press box. (top left) John Ayers and Randy Cross await the start of Super Bowl. (bottom left) Jack Reynolds advises Bobby Leopold as Ronnie Lott watches. (top right) Eric Wright sits quietly; cheerleaders look happy. (bottom right) Norb Hecker tells linebackers what Bengals will do.

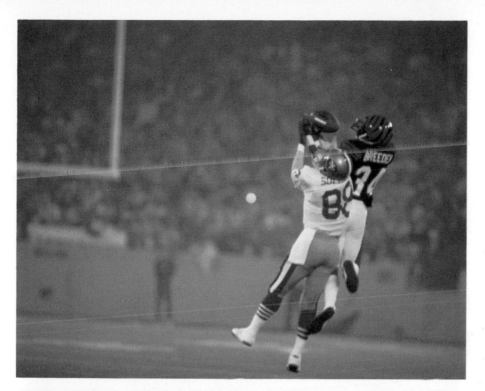

(left) Joe Montana fades to pass in the Super Bowl behind blocking of Randy Cross, left, and Fred Quillan, right. (top right) Fred Solomon outduels Cincinnati cornerback Louis Breeden to make over-the-head catch. (bottom right) Dwight Clark is brought down after catching pass for good gain.

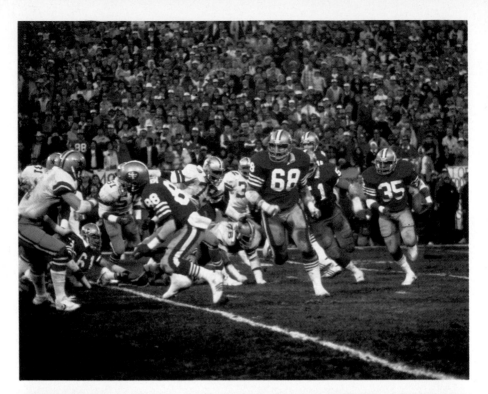

(upper left), Fred Solomon, John Ayers and Randy Cross lead
Lenvil Elliott on a sweep against Dallas. (lower left) Solomon
gains 12 on reverse that helped set up winning touchdown in
NFC championship game. (right) Joe Montana scores the first
touchdown on a quarterback sneak in the Super Bowl.

(left) Earl Cooper leaps high in joy after scoring touchdown on Joe Montana pass in Super Bowl. (top right) Charle Young is upended after catching pass in Super Bowl — but he hangs on to the ball. (bottom right). The 49er defense stacks up Cincinnati's Pete Johnson at the goal line in third quarter.

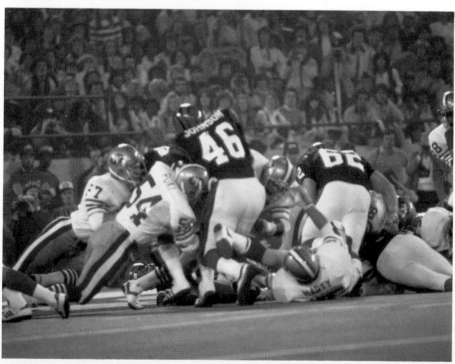

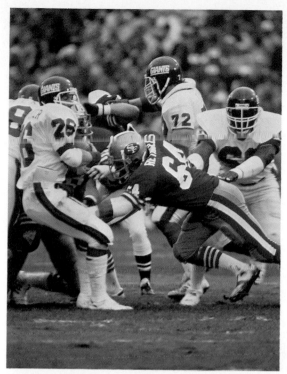

(left) Ray Wersching kicks clinching field goal in Super Bowl. (top right) Jack Reynolds makes tackle against Giants in playoff. (bottom right) Fred Dean closes on Dallas QB Danny White in championship game.

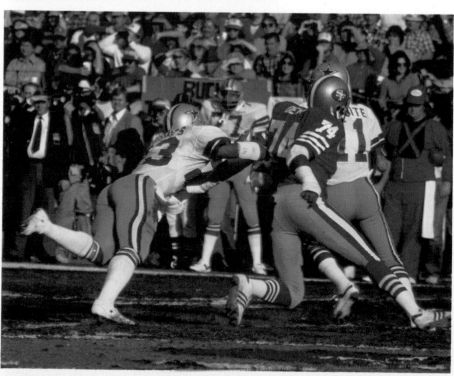

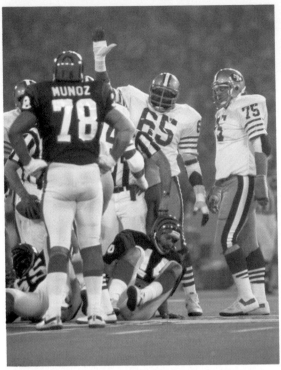

(top left) Archie Reese makes key quarterback sack of Ken Anderson in Super Bowl. (bottom left) Eric Wright intercepts Anderson pass in closing minutes. (right) Ronnie Lott and Dwight Hicks leap high in celebration as the 49ers win the Super Bowl.

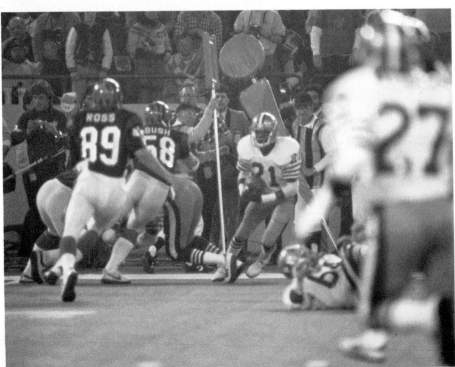

(left) Charle Young signals touchdown after Joe Montana sneaks over in Super Bowl. (top right) NFL commissioner Pete Rozelle hands Vince Lombardi Trophy to 49er owner Ed DeBartolo Jr., as Bill Walsh claps. (bottom right) Forty-Niner fans show their feelings. (overleaf) Fans throng Market Street for 49er parade.

10

RAMS FALL AGAIN

The Los Angeles Rams were having a quarterback controversy. That was hardly news; the Rams *always* have a quarterback controversy. In the fifties, it had been Bob Waterfield and Norm Van Brocklin, and then, Van Brocklin and Billy Wade. More recently, it had been Pat Haden and whoever else was there: James Harris, Ron Jaworski, Vince Ferragamo. Now, it was Haden and Dan Pastorini, formerly of the Houston Oilers and Oakland Raiders.

The first Ram quarterback controversy didn't really hurt the team because the coach could choose between two quality players. What difference did it make if he sent Waterfield or Van Brocklin in to throw that 80-yard touchdown pass?

But Haden and Pastorini weren't in that class. Each had significant weaknesses.

Haden was smart, a Rhodes scholar in fact, a good leader and a good athlete, but because of his size he had been fighting an uphill battle since he joined the Rams.

In an off-season conversation a couple of years ago, Haden demonstrated to me that, with his straight overhand throwing style, he actually released the ball only a couple of inches lower than taller quarterbacks who threw with a three-quarters or sidearm motion.

But the question was less whether Haden could throw over defensive linemen than if he could see over them. True, Johnny Unitas was only a couple of inches taller than Haden, but he had played in an era when the linemen weren't so tall. Fran Tarkenton, perhaps just an inch taller, had been a scrambler who had rolled out so he could see downfield. Haden was more of a classic dropback passer and a good one; John McKay had called him the best college quarterback he had coached.

Pastorini had everything Haden lacked physically. He could throw the ball accurately and as far as any quarterback in the game. He had the size scouts look for in a pro quarterback, and he was a courageous player who had played with injuries throughout his career. But Pastorini was a very erratic personality, often in trouble. He had fought with a sportswriter, he had run his car into a tree, he had been hurt racing a speedboat.

Pastorini had been released by Oakland earlier in the year for unexplained reasons, though some thought it was because he had told Oakland owner Al Davis that he wasn't willing to be a reserve behind both Jim Plunkett and second-year quarterback Marc Wilson. Others thought it was because of his off-field behavior. But Davis isn't a man who cuts players because of their actions away from the field. Davis obviously felt Pastorini couldn't help the Raiders, and Davis makes very few mistakes on player judgments.

Even with that background, though, Pastorini would be starting for the Rams against the 49ers. Rams coach Ray Malavasi felt he had to try something; the Rams were 5-6 and very close to being mathematically eliminated in the NFC West.

The 49ers had troubles of their own. Because of his bruised sternum, Fred Dean couldn't play, and the fourth quarter of the Cleveland loss had shown what a difference Dean's absence made to the 49er defense.

There were a lot of questions about the San Francisco offense, too. The 49ers, as Walsh pointed out, had been an opportunistic team on offense, scoring when they had to in every game but the Cleveland loss, but they'd gotten by with a minmum of production since the Dallas win. They had scored only two offensive touchdowns against Los Angeles, Pittsburgh, and Atlanta, a single TD against Green Bay, and none against Cleveland—only seven touchdowns in five games.

Clearly, they had been leaning too much on their defense, and their defense wouldn't be able to shut down the Rams this time, without Dean, as it had in the first game. Had the bubble burst?

It hadn't, but it took the 49ers three-plus hours and the most exciting game yet to prove that. The first game between the teams had been thrilling because of the incredible fourth-quarter tension and pressure of the 49er defense. This one was a wide-open offensive show, with enough spectacular plays to mount a lengthy highlight film. The lead changed hands four times; three times the game was tied, and first the Rams then the 49ers performed late-game heroics when all seemed lost.

The game started slowly, with Ray Wersching's 47-yard field goal for the 49ers the only scoring in the first quarter.

The tempo picked up considerably in the second quarter. First, Frank Corral kicked a 44-yard field goal to tie the game, and then the Rams drove 80 yards on 11 plays to take the lead. Pastorini hit running back Wendell Tyler on a 22-yard pass on third-and-seven for the touchdown.

The 49ers came back with an explosive drive, 74 yards in just five plays. Montana passed for 44 and 28 yards to Fred Solomon for most of the yardage, and Johnny Davis surged over for the last yard and the TD.

Before the half, the Rams came back with another 80-yard drive, this one taking 13 plays. A pass interference call against Saladin Martin gave the Rams a first down on the seven. Two plays later Mike Guman threw to Preston Dennard on a run-pass option for the touchdown. Corral's PAT gave the Rams a 17-10 halftime advantage.

That lead lasted only 18 seconds into the third quarter. Amos Lawrence caught the second-half kickoff on his eight, broke a tackle by Joe Harris at the 29 and another by LeRoy Irvin at the 34, and them outraced everybody for a touchdown.

This was the first kick return for a touchdown by the 49ers all season, and an especially gratifying one for Lawrence, who had been so close to breaking away in two other games.

Lawrence had been a late acquisition for the 49ers, coming to the team in September in a trade with the San Diego Chargers, who couldn't reach a contract agreement with their fourth-round draft pick. Though Walsh thought highly of Lawrence's future with the club, that late arrival had kept him from being used for more than an occasional play from scrimmage.

"He really needs a training camp," said Walsh. "He played in an entirely different formation [the I formation] in college, and it's been a tough learning experience for him here.

"Maybe if we had a simple offense, he'd be able to fit in better, but he's had to learn things week to week. He'll learn a few plays one week, and then have to go to another set the next week.

"Because he doesn't know the offense, we haven't been able to use him much. We couldn't be sure he'd be in the right place on a pass pattern, for instance, and in these close games, that could be critical.

"But, I think he can be a real help. He's not terribly elusive, but he's got quick feet and he kind of slides off tacklers. And I think he has a real potential as a pass receiver coming out of the backfield. It's possible that in a couple of years, maybe even next year, he could be the kind of guy who catches fifty, sixty balls."

Lawrence's return began the best stretch for the 49ers that November afternoon, as they scored 17 points without answer from the Rams.

The Niners next score came from Wersching, who kicked a 34-yard field goal after a long drive—with a 23-yard pass from Montana to Dwight Clark and a 14-yard run by Davis—had bogged down at the Los Angeles 17.

Then Ronnie Lott showed the mental awareness that, as much as his tremendous physical ability, sets him apart from other defensive backs.

"I try to pick up everything that happens on a football field," he says. "The body movements of other players, the way that they carry themselves. Football is a game of emotions. Everybody shows them. You can pick up what's going through people's minds."

On this occasion the Rams' Billy Waddy ran a semi-curl in front of Lott. Waddy was wide open, but Pastorini didn't see him. Waddy ran straight to Pastorini after the play had ended and before the Rams huddled. "I figured he was telling Pastorini about the play," said Lott.

Waddy was, and Pastorini came back to him on the next play. Lott was prepared; he cut in front of Waddy to grab the interception and returned it 25 yards for a touchdown.

It was Lott's third interception touchdown of the season, tying an NFL rookie record and equaling the 49ers' *career* record for interceptions returned for touchdowns.

"I don't want to just play a position," Lott says. "I want to make big plays. When you get the ball, don't be satisfied with that. You try to score. When you make an interception and don't do anything with it—that's nothing."

That interception caused Malavasi to change quarterbacks, and Haden came off the bench firing. He immediately drove the Rams 80 yards in nine plays to cut the 49er lead to 27-24. The key play was his 43-yard pass to Drew Hill, and he got the touchdown with a two-yard flip to Walt Arnold.

Wersching gave the 49ers a little more breathing room by hitting his seventh straight field goal, this one from 32 yards, with 4:50 elapsed in the fourth quarter.

The ensuing kickoff backed the Rams to their own ten, and then Haden started an excruciating drive which typified the entire game: sudden ups and downs, accompanied by nail-biting tension.

At least three times, the 49ers seemed to have the Rams stopped. And three times, the Rams came back. On third-and-18 from the Los Angeles 29, Haden hit Dennard on a 22-yard pass that gave the Rams a first down on the San Francisco 49. On third-and-five on the next series, Haden hit Tyler for a seven-yard gain for the first. And on fourth-and-three from the San Francisco 30, Haden hit Guman for a 14-yard gain.

A pass interference call against Willie Harper brought the ball to the one, and Tyler scored from there. Corral's PAT put the Rams on top, 31-30.

The tension-filled drive had consumed eight minutes. The 49ers had only 1:51 left, and the depressing turn of events would probably have beaten a lesser team. "The 49ers have never had poise before," recalled Jack Reynolds, later, who knew what it had been like in his days with the Rams. "I remember in '79, they had us on the ropes, but they couldn't put us away. A lot of times, they would have just folded their tent."

Not anymore. Now the 49ers had Joe Montana and Ray Wersching, two consummate clutch performers. From the time Wersching had joined the club in 1977 until the end of the 1980 season, the 49ers had won only 15 games, and his kicks had decided six of them at the end of the fourth quarter or in overtime. So far in 1981, his field goals had been the difference in four 49er wins.

Montana's trademark had always been his ability to bring a team back. At Notre Dame, he had done it six times during his career, the most spectacular being the Cotton Bowl in his senior year. Notre Dame trailed Houston, 34-12, going into the fourth quarter, but Montana's heroics produced a 35-34 victory, the winning touchdown coming on his pass to Kris Haines on the last play of the game.

He had done much the same with the 49ers, and had come to be known for his poise, especially in the last two minutes, the time that separates the great quarterbacks from the average ones. "Most quarterbacks lose control right around here," says

Walsh. "They're trying to think of everything, and they can't think."

Montana, in contrast, shuts out everything but the relevant issues. The crowd noise doesn't intrude. He doesn't panic. He sees everything on the field and makes the play. He seems as calm as most quarterbacks are early in the second quarter of an exhibition game.

This time, he knew he had to drive the team just far enough to give Wersching a chance to kick a field goal. "We knew that if we got within 50 yards, Ray would kick it," said Randy Cross.

The winning drive began at the 49ers' 20. Three short completions and one run got the 49ers to their own 42, where they had second-and-one with 1:09 left.

A Montana pass on second down went just off Clark's fingertips. On third down, he had to throw the ball away because his receiver, Solomon, was covered.

Fourth down. One yard to go. The game was on the line. Walsh called for a sweep, but the Rams put two safeties up on the line, a defense that had stopped the sweep effectively earlier in the game.

Montana changed the play, calling an audible for a play where right guard Cross pulls out to block the defensive lineman coming between left guard John Ayers and center Fred Quillan, and Paul Hofer rams into the hole. "I was scared," admitted Montana, but Hofer got two yards and the first down.

Three plays later, on third-and-five, Montana threw to Clark for 16 yards, giving the 49ers a first down on the Los Angeles 35. They were almost within field goal range now.

Then Montana improvised. Solomon and Clark were both on the left side, with Solomon flanked outside Clark. The quarterback thought the Rams' defense would be vulnerable if Clark ran ten yards deep and cut left. The 49ers hadn't run that play during the season and hadn't even practiced it since training camp, but Montana was right. Solomon cleared the area by going deep, and Montana threw to Clark at the 25, who then battled for five more yards.

Only 23 seconds remained, and the 49ers had just one timeout left. An incomplete pass stopped the clock. Earl Cooper got one yard into the center of the line. Montana let the clock run down to two seconds, so the game would end with the field goal attempt, and then used the Niners final timeout.

Montana came into the huddle and said, "This has to be perfect." It was. Cross, who snaps the ball for placekicks, put the ball back on line, Montana put it down, and Wersching kicked it through. The 49ers had won, 33-31.

It wasn't pretty, but it was a win, and the 49ers had beaten the Rams twice in the same season for the first time since 1965. The Rams, at 5-7, were out of the race, and the 49ers were only one win from clinching the divisional title.

"I'm in shock about what we're doing," admitted Reynolds. "I won't say we're for real. We're lucky, very lucky, but it has been a very pleasant experience, very gratifying. That drive showed we have real character and a backbone."

And Walsh had a word of advice for the losing coach. "Pat Haden is a great quarterback. I cannot understand the controversy."

11

THE 49ERS CLINCH

It had been nine years since the 49ers had won a division title, but when they clinched the NFC West with a 17-10 win over the New York Giants the next Sunday, they acted as if it were just another ball game.

Oh, there was a little ceremony as some players, led by Ronnie Lott, carried coach Bill Walsh off the field, but that ended after a few steps. Paul Hofer seemed to be the only player really hit by the emotion of the moment. "When those last seconds were ticking off the clock, it was a phenomenal feeling," he said. "To be able to watch the fans who have stuck with us for so long, and the guys who have been through the hard times—it was just great."

In the dressing room the players were quiet and subdued. Their post-game ritual was the same as always: they said a prayer, listened to a few words from Walsh, waited for the phone call from owner Edward DeBartolo, Jr., talked to the press.

There was no champagne, not even any beer; NFL rules prohibit alcohol in the dressing rooms, but more excited teams have been known to overlook that rule.

The 49ers were calm for a couple of reasons. One was that they had anticipated both their win, and the winning of a divisional title. They had, after all, been leading the division for most of the season and by a good margin much of that time. Only a complete reversal could have cost them the title.

But more importantly, for the first time they were allowing

themselves to think of the ultimate, the Super Bowl.

"I think everybody realizes how far we have an opportunity to go," said Keith Fahnhorst. "It feels good to have it wrapped up, but none of us are going to be satisfied with just the Western Division championship.

"The way it was right after the game, you'd have thought this was old hat for us, like it was the seventh time in the last eight years we'd won it."

Randy Cross observed that winning the division title after leading for so long was "almost anticlimactic," and added, "We've been winning and winning and winning. We've been hanging on for the whole year. Everybody outside of the team has been waiting for something to go wrong, but I think maybe we've proved something."

Jack Reynolds was the one 49er who was accustomed to winning; with the Rams, he had played on seven division winners in eight years. But Reynolds is the classic pessimist; to him, the glass is always half-empty. Teammates feel the more worried Reynolds is about an upcoming game, the more likely they are to win.

"We were very fortunate to beat the New Orleans Saints and we were very fortunate to beat the Chicago Bears," said Reynolds, "and those aren't two powerhouse teams. I don't know how we're doing it but as long as we're winning, that's all right."

Walsh was equally low-key. With tongue in cheek he told the media, "It appears we've won our division." Not everybody caught the humor in the remark; one columnist wrote some palpable nonsense about Walsh being worried about a jinx.

Walsh *was* worried about his running, even in victory. Montana had been forced to pass 39 times, far too many, because the 49er running game could do little against the defensively tough Giants. Indeed, Montana had the longest 49er run of the day, 20 yards.

"I think we're playing at close to one hundred percent efficiency week after week," he said. "That's almost unheard of in the NFL in recent years. But we don't dominate anybody because we don't have that big runner."

Even while savoring the championship, Walsh was thinking of what he could do to solve the running back problem the next year. Because of their record, the 49ers would be drafting low, and Walsh thought he might have to trade a couple of picks to move higher in the first round. "To be honest," he said, "I thought we'd have a fairly high drafting position next year. But I prefer this."

Still, though the 49ers treated the win rather lightly, the title was a considerable accomplishment. They were the first team in the entire NFL to clinch a division title, and they hadn't backed in. They had beaten their chief rivals, Los Angeles and Atlanta, when they had to.

Their ten wins equaled the best a San Francisco team had ever done in the NFL, and represented as many wins as the team had had in its three previous seasons combined! This year was only the second winning season since 1972.

Even the way the win over the Giants was accomplished was a good sign. This was precisely the kind of dull, patternless game the 49ers had lost so often in the recent past. This time they won it.

Because of the importance of the game, there was apprehension in the 49er locker room before the players came out, but that didn't show in the early play. As had been true so many times this season, the 49ers got on the board first and never trailed thereafter.

The first touchdown came after Dwight Hicks returned an interception 54 yards to the New York 15. It was slow going for the 49ers from that point, but Johnny Davis finally pushed across from the one on the drive's seventh play.

Another break, this one a Keena Turner recovery of a fumble by Giants running back Rob Carpenter, set up the second San Francisco touchdown. The 49ers started on the New York 40 this time, and Montana's 20-yard run on a quarterback draw produced the touchdown.

Montana's run was the longest for a 49er since the second game of the season and the third longest of the year, a telling indictment of the San Francisco running attack.

That lack of a running attack kept this game from being the blowout it really should have been. A minute later, Carlton Williamson recovered still another fumble for the 49ers, and a touchdown, maybe even a field goal, would have wrapped up the victory against a Giants' team long on defense but short on offense.

But the Giants stiffened this time. The 49ers got no points out of this possession, and the game was a struggle from that point.

Just before the half, Joe Danelo boomed through a 52-yard field goal to make it 14-3 at halftime. A scoreless third quarter followed, with neither team being able to move the ball with any consistency.

Then, on the first play of the fourth quarter, Rob

Carpenter scored on a three-yard run that capped a 76-yard drive for the Giants, drawing them to within 14-10 after Danelo's PAT.

But all season the 49ers had been able to come up with a sustained scoring drive when they most needed it, and now they did it again, saving a win that seemed in jeopardy. Joe Montana calmly took his team from the San Francisco 22 to the New York one, using up seven minutes in the drive.

At the 23 they faced a fourth-and-one; Walsh went for the first down, which Davis got, gaining two yards. But when the 49ers came down to fourth down again, this time on the one, Walsh went for the field goal. A delay-of-game penalty pushed the 49ers back five yards, but reliable Ray Wersching boomed a 23-yarder.

That forced the Giants to try to play catchup, which they don't do very well. New York got the ball three more times...and failed to make a single first down.

Finally, Williamson intercepted a Scott Brunner pass to end the game and clinch the divisional title for the 49ers. The fans, who had been waiting a long, long time for this moment, poured out of the stands, onto the field, singing, dancing, screaming their joy. Most of them seemed to have pennants, banners, or signs of some description, and the party on the field and later in the parking lot probably went on longer than the game itself.

The fans were deliriously happy.

Even if the players weren't.

12

REVENGE FOR WALSH

Not the least of Bill Walsh's coaching abilities is his knowledge of which psychological buttons to push in getting his team ready to play.

His approach at Stanford was an intellectual one. He knew his players were more intelligent than the average, which meant they could absorb his system quickly, but were likely to become rapidly bored by the repetitious football drills. So Walsh made his practices short and snappy, a model of economy, to lessen the boredom factor. He challenged his players to learn a system of far more complexity than anything they had known before. And he treated them like adults, not just football robots. His approach worked perfectly.

With the 49ers, he was dealing with players who were less intelligent and less sophisticated than those at Standford (with some obvious exceptions). He had told me when he took the job that he thought it would take three years to install a system he had essentially installed in a year at Stanford—and this was the third year.

He had adjusted his approach accordingly. He played heavily on the underdog theme, as in the preparation for Pittsburgh, for instance. If an opposing coach said anything that could be construed as denigration of the 49ers, it went up on the walls of the locker room at Redwood City. That infuriated some football writers, who thought of it as a high school tactic, but it wasn't aimed at writers.

As the 49ers prepared for Cincinnati, Walsh didn't have to worry about psychological ploys. His team knew what had to be done. "The players know that he wants this game bad," said Joe Montana. "I don't think it needs to be said."

But Walsh managed this time to con the Bengals, their coaching staff, and also some of the national media. He talked of how good the Bengals were, certainly no exaggeration. He talked of how much Cincinnati needed the game, which was also true. Though the Bengals had the same record as the 49ers—10-3—they were in a treacherous spot. If they lost to the 49ers, they could slip to only one game ahead of the Steelers, who had won three in a row, and they had to face the Steelers in Pittsburgh the next Sunday. Thus, a slight slump at this point and the Bengals could conceivably be tied with the Steelers.

Walsh also pointed out that the 49ers had clinched their title, and he implied that they might let down somewhat in the wake of that triumph. He added that he was looking for a spot to give playing time to reserves like quarterback Guy Benjamin and running back Amos Lawrence, who hadn't had much chance to play.

Walsh didn't say that he would start either player, or even that he would play his reserves a lot in this game, but some people leaped to that conclusion, the most conspicuous being Howard Cosell.

On ABC Radio's "Speaking of Sports," Cosell said, "Forty-Niner coach Bill Walsh says he'll play second-string players against Cincinnati. Because the 49ers have already clinched a playoff berth, that will give him a good excuse for losing, which the 49ers will do. It's wrong to play second-stringers. I know the Tony LaRussa theory—'Save your players and win when it counts.' The 49ers want to win in the playoffs, but it's still wrong."

That helped convince the Bengals that the 49ers wouldn't be at their best, but anybody who thought Walsh wouldn't go all out in this game didn't know the man at all.

Walsh was still resentful because he had been passed over for the head coaching job of the Bengals when Paul Brown had retired in 1975, even though he much preferred to be coaching and living in the Bay Area.

As offensive coordinator Walsh had been responsible for much of the Bengals' success from 1969 to 1975. He had been widely regarded as the heir apparent to Brown. But when the time came to name a successor after the 1975 season, Brown chose Bill Johnson, another assistant. The angry and disappointed Walsh left and joined the San Diego Charger staff.

Nobody ever knew quite why Walsh was passed over. Brown's one public statement, that he thought Walsh would want to return to California, was nonsense. Despite Walsh's admitted, and understandable, preference for California, his priority was a head coaching job on the pro level, which Brown fully understood. If all Walsh wanted was to return to California, he could have done that at any time by settling for an assistant's job, as he eventually did with San Diego.

Paul Brown is a curious man, capable of extremely vindictive actions. He harbors petty jealousies and smoldering anger. (In the book he did with Jack Clary, "PB: The Paul Brown Story," darts of rage fly off the pages.) It's possible that Walsh, unknowingly, did something that offended Brown. It's also possible, as some have suggested, that Brown thought Walsh was too scholarly to be an effective head coach.

It's probably more likely that just the opposite is true: Brown thought Walsh would be too *good* a head coach, which might cause people to forget how great a coach Brown himself had been.

There is no questioning the ability of Paul Brown, who's in the Pro Football Hall of Fame. He won on every level: high school, college, and pro. He took four straight AAC titles with the Cleveland Browns, and another three NFL titles and seven divisional titles. He turned the Bengals, an expansion team, into a division champion in three years; the Bengals were 11-3 in Brown's final season. During his 25 years as a pro coach, his teams won 213 games and lost only 104.

Paul Brown and his coaching innovations have had a tremendous influence on the game. He was the first, for instance, to use intelligence tests to determine a player's learning potential; to use notebooks and classroom techniques; to set up complete film clip statistical studies and grade his players from those studies. He was also the first coach to keep his players together in a hotel before a home game; others had done it only before games on the road.

Brown didn't want anybody to forget his contributions to football. The game is his life. The five years he spent out of football, after being fired by Cleveland owner Art Modell at the end of the 1962 season, were spent in La Jolla, California, the garden spot of the world. But Brown was miserable, a fish out of water, and he leaped at the chance to get back into pro football with the Bengals in 1968.

By selecting Johnson as his replacement, Brown could be

assured that his own legend wouldn't be tarnished. Johnson had some early success as a carry-over from Brown, but the Bengals went downhill so quickly that nobody could doubt that it had been Paul Brown's coaching that had made them successful: from 10-4 in Johnson's first year to 8-6 his second, and 0-5 in the portion of the third season he lasted before being fired.

As Johnson's replacement, Brown hired Homer Rice, a knowledgeable football man but one lacking the charisma a head coach needs; Rice was 4-7 in a partial season, 4-12 in his one full year.

Significantly it wasn't until criticism of the Bengals started to be directed at Brown, for dictating policy to his coaches and dominating the organization, that he finally hired a strong coach, Forrest Gregg.

Now Walsh was returning to Cincinnati, eager to prove to Brown and the Cincinnati fans that it had been a serious error to bypass him. His task wouldn't be easy. During their bad years the Bengals had been in a position to draft some excellent players, and many people in football thought Cincinnati was now the best team in the league. Their biggest star was quarterback Ken Anderson, whom Walsh had made into a top-flight pro player.

Anderson had played for small Augustana College in Illinois, where he had caught the eye of Brown's son, Pete, the personnel director. Another Brown son, Mike, then the assistant general manager, scouted him and was also impressed; then Walsh gave him a tryout and added his approval.

"He was a great, raw talent," says Walsh. "He was the biggest player on his team and the fastest."

The Browns grabbed Anderson on the third round in 1971, one pick before Atlanta; Falcons' coach Norm Van Brocklin was also set to draft the quarterback.

Walsh worked and worked with Anderson on the physical aspects of a quarterback's job, drilling him endlessly on such basics as dropping back into the pocket. Anderson had been a sprint-out passer in college but he soon became a classic pro passer, though he was often able to run for yardage when his protection broke down.

Walsh also worked on building up Anderson's confidence. One example came in Anderson's first pro year when he replaced starter Virgil Carter, who had hurt his shoulder, in a game against Green Bay. Trying to keep a drive going in the final seconds, the rookie quarterback was forced out of the pocket and tried to run for a first down. He came up short and the Packers won, 20-17.

As Anderson stepped into the locker room, he was met by Paul Brown. "Well, Anderson," said Brown, "there's another game you lost for us."

Walsh immediately took Anderson aside and talked to him for a long time to make certain Anderson's confidence wouldn't be destroyed, either by the game or Brown's remark.

Bob Trumpy, then a receiver for the Bengals and now a radio-TV announcer, noted another way that Walsh built up Anderson's confidence. "Walsh gave the receivers things to help Anderson," says Trumpy. "Even when he scrambled, there was someone for him to throw to. It was all set up. He always had a place to go."

"It's hard for me to describe Bill Walsh as a teacher," says Anderson, "because I think of him above all as a friend. We worked together and we spent time together off the field. We've kept in touch over the years. I guess the greatest things he gave me were solid, fundamental techniques and confidence in what I was doing."

Now Anderson would be trying to beat his friend, and vice versa.

The Bengals-49er game would be a tough, physical one. "It was emphasized all week long that we had to outhit them," said Randy Cross. "It was another of those games, like Pittsburgh, where you could feel that in the whole mood of the team."

The 49ers would force six turnovers—three interceptions and three fumbles—by a team that had a league and season low of 15 turnovers going into the game. Two of the fumbles were caused by jarring tackles by Ronnie Lott. And in the third period, Anderson was knocked out of the game with a bent toe after a dramatic sack by Bobby Leopold.

"Our team hits as hard as any in football," said Walsh.

The pattern of the game was established early. On Cincinnati's first possession, Anderson tried to pass to Isaac Curtis on third-and-seven from the San Francisco 43. Lott batted the ball into the air with his right hand and then caught it as it came back down.

After that, the 49ers drove 66 yards to score in 15 plays, with Montana throwing to Bill Ring for the final four yards. It was Joe's first touchdown pass in four games.

As with all the turnovers that followed, Lott's interception came when the 49ers were in a formation aimed at stopping the pass. Frequently the Bengals were forced into obvious passing situations, enabling the 49ers to control the game's tempo.

"All year we've been forcing teams to make turnovers," Anderson said as he left the stadium on crutches after the game. "Today we were forced to make them."

Sometimes the 49ers used their "nickel" defense (an extra defensive back in, a linebacker out). Sometimes they went further, adding a sixth defensive back to replace the second linebacker, because of tight end Dan Ross. "We weren't sure that we could handle Ross with a linebacker," said defensive coordinator Chuck Studley.

Whatever defense the 49ers played, they went after the Bengals. "We go out there with the idea of getting the ball for our offense," said Lott. "We've got an aggressive secondary. We're always looking for the ball. A couple of times today, if we were just looking to make the play instead of stealing the ball, they could have had completions."

Late in the second quarter the Bengals finally got on the scoreboard with a 30-yard field goal by Jim Breech, but it could have been worse for the Niners. One play before Carlton Williamson had knocked down a pass to Steve Kreider in the end zone, preventing a touchdown.

There was only 2:26 left in the half when the 49ers got the ball on their 20 following the Cincinnati kickoff—but that was Joe Montana time. Montana took his team 80 yards to score with just two seconds remaining in the half.

The key play of the drive came when Montana ran for 13 yards on a third-and-ten situation from the San Francisco 49; the 49ers got another 15 yards when the Bengals were called for unnecessary roughness.

The touchdown was a beauty. Dwight Clark was double-covered in the rear of the end zone but Montana was able to loft his pass over safety Bryan Hicks, and Clark kept his feet just inbounds for the touchdown.

The 49ers scored once more, midway through the fourth quarter, going 40 yards after Dwight Hicks recovered a fumble by Ross, induced by a Lott tackle. Montana ran for the final yard. Three touchdowns for San Francisco, one field goal for Cincinnati: 21-3.

In the Cincinnati dressing room, Gregg told the media after the game that he had noticed as early as Wednesday that the team was flat. He had known, he said, that the Bengals wouldn't play well.

"Can you believe that nobody asked him *why* they were flat for such an important game?" Walsh asked me later.

No.

Walsh had a lot to be happy with, and he flashed a big smile at reporters after the game. "I think it was a hard-fought game and the better team won," he said. "It was a pleasant victory, in particular for some of us who have represented the Bengals in the past."

The 49ers had won without star wide receiver Fred Solomon, out with a bruised kidney. They had gotten a big day from running back Earl Cooper, who had rushed for 57 yards in the second half, a major factor in protecting the lead. "Earl would be one of the premier runners in the NFL if he could run on artificial turf all the time," said Walsh.

Their 11-3 mark was the best in the NFL, and they were assured of hosting at least the first playoff game: the "home swamp" advantage, the *Chronicle*'s Ira Miller called it.

Significantly, the 49ers' most impressive wins had come over the two strongest teams they'd faced, Dallas and Cincinnati. Against the Bengals, the 49ers' defense had held the league's second most productive offense to a field goal. The Bengals, in fact, had gotten no further than the San Francisco 35 in the second half, until the final two minutes, when the game was out of reach.

And, yes, Howard, Bill Walsh did play his reserves—in the final six minutes.

13

THE NFL'S BEST RECORD

The year before, the 49ers had been playing for pride going into the final two games, trying to salvage something from a disappointing season.

This year they were playing for pride, too, but of a quite different sort: they wanted to finish with the best record in the league. Considering they had the worst record just two years before, such a turnaround would be an almost unparalleled feat, though the Chicago Cardinals had once done it. They came from the NFL's worst record (1-9) in 1945 to the best (9-3) in 1947.

For the Niners, the more practical matter of field advantage was also involved. If San Francisco won their last two games, they were assured of the home field for both the playoff round *and* the championsip game, assuming they won the playoff game. If the 49ers finished at 13-3, Dallas was the only team that could equal that record, and the fact that the 49ers had beaten the Cowboys in the regular season would be the tie-breaker in deciding the game site.

Playing at home would be an advantage because of fan support and the fact that the players' lives and practice schedules would not have any unusual disruptions. The field itself, getting more and more beat up, wasn't an advantage. Indeed, there were times when coach Bill Walsh thought it was a disadvantage.

"We have to play on it ten times a year," Walsh noted. "Other teams only have to worry about it once.

"There's nothing we can run that other teams can't, and it really restricts us. People look at our team and say, 'Where's your running? Where are your offensive statistics?' Well, a lot of that is the field, because there's really so little you can do. You can't run wide, you can't cut sharply."

It wasn't supposed to happen that way. "I had meetings with the people in charge before the start of the season," said Walsh. "The engineers were there, too. They had all the plans laid out and it was supposed to be a great field. Obviously, it didn't turn out exactly that way.

"I'm sure the people living a quarter of a mile away have better lawns. Maybe we should call them in and have them plant the field."

* * * *

The biggest play of the game against Houston came on the 49ers' first play from scrimmage, when Earl Cooper caught a screen pass, knocked over a couple of defenders, and bolted 41 yards. Though the play was wasted because the 49er drive was eventually stopped on fourth down at the Houston one, it was a sign that Cooper was playing back to his rookie year form.

Cooper had been the first draft pick the year before, and Walsh had made some extravagant comments about him, comparing him to Chuck Foreman as a combination runner-receiver.

It seemed that Walsh was right when Cooper rushed for 720 yards, on a 4.2 average, and caught 83 passes to lead the NFC and set a club record as a rookie.

But everything had gone wrong in 1981. At his best, Cooper was not a powerful inside runner, despite his size. He needed to be able to get some running room to make his gliding style effective. In 1981, he seemed tentative in his movements, and he was often tackled before he really got going. He was being used less and less, and when he was in the game, it was usually as a receiver, not a runner.

"I think the field bothered Earl a lot," said Walsh. "He couldn't get the footing he needed. And, to be honest, the blocking wasn't always quite good enough, either. Our players would hold their blocks but they wouldn't blast anybody away. That kind of block was enough for a runner who really slammed into the hole, but Earl isn't that kind of runner. I think it helped Earl when we got Johnny Davis, because that took the pressure off him to run inside,"

But Cooper had been coming back gradually. The week before, he had had his best day. Against Houston he was even better, gaining 115 yards rushing and receiving, all the more significant because it was achieved on a sloppy field, not the artificial turf on which he excelled. Cooper's teammates gave him a game ball for the first time since the first game of his rookie year, and he credited Walsh for his turnaround.

"I think he handled it well," said Cooper. "He didn't make me go out and try to get it all back in one game. He put me in to run around end, or catch passes, just using me to get my confidence back."

Walsh had deliberately downplayed Cooper's problems, too, seldom saying anything for publication while encouraging the second-year back privately. It helped, of course, that the 49ers took off so spectacularly because that took attention away from Cooper's failures.

It meant a lot, Joe Montana felt, to have Cooper back in form. "When Earl was in a slump," said Montana, "it was pass automatically when he came into a game. We tried to disguise a lot of it, but it didn't work out. We'd bring Johnny Davis in at the goal line, and you could just follow Johnny and that's where the ball's going to be. That's the way it had been."

With Cooper playing well, the 49ers showed a more varied attack down by the goal line. Their three third-quarter touchdowns, after a scoreless first half, came on a two-yard run inside by Ricky Patton, a three-yard run outside by Cooper, and a two-yard pass to Dwight Clark, who caught five passes to give him a club record 84 for the season.

With the game well in hand, Walsh put in Guy Benjamin for Montana in the fourth quarter. Benjamin, with his first chance all season to pass, completed seven of nine and got the final 49er touchdown with a 27-yard pass to Mike Wilson.

Earl Campbell, held to just 45 yards in 18 carries by the 49er defense, got Houston's only score with a one-yard plunge with only 47 seconds left. Toni Fritsch's PAT was blocked by Dwaine Board, and the 49ers won, 28-6.

* * * *

Because Dallas had lost to the New York Giants the day before, the 49ers had already clinched the home field for the NFC championship game before they even took the field against the Saints in New Orleans on the last Sunday of the season. That made Walsh's primary concern avoiding key injuries, and took Montana out of the game after only 19 minutes. Joe had already thrown two touchdown passes.

The game wouldn't have been close except for two consecutive fumbled kicks late in the first quarter. Fred Solomon fumbled a punt; the Saints recovered on the 18 and went on to score. Amos Lawrence fumbled the ensuing kickoff (twice!); the Saints recovered on the seven this time and scored again.

The 49ers had a chance to score just before halftime, but Benjamin threw an interception that he later called "the stupidest play of my life." The play started as a screen pass; when Benjamin saw the Saints had the play covered, he tried to throw to Clark in the end zone, behind two defenders.

"I thought I saw something," said Benjamin, "but when you think, you don't throw it. You only throw it when you know."

But Benjamin later redeemed himself. After the Saints had taken a 17-14 lead with a third-quarter field goal, Guy took the 49ers on a seven-play, 79-yard drive in which he completed all three passes he threw, one of them against a blitz, for 48 yards. "I thought he moved the ballclub well," Clark said. "It's nice to know that if Joe should get hurt, we've got a capable quarterback who can come in."

Interestingly, Benjamin had played for the Saints the year before. "It was a fun game because I knew practically everybody on the field," he said.

Sloppy though it was, the win gave the 49ers some individual and team satisfactions. Clark caught one pass to raise his team record to 85, and he became the second straight 49er to win the NFC receiving title (Cooper won the previous year).

Their 13 wins were a franchise record, exceeding the 12 by the 1948 club, in the All-America Conference. Their sixth straight road win was another club record, and their six-game margin over second-place Atlanta was the third biggest spread in NFL history. Only unbeaten Miami (1972) and the Rams (1975) had had seven-game margins.

"We can take tremendous pride in having the best record in the NFL," said Walsh. "Regardless of what happens in the playoffs, that's a significant achievement."

14

GIANTS BAFFLED

Nobody knew Bill Walsh better than John Ralston did. At one time Walsh had been an assistant on Ralston's staff at Stanford. More recently, Ralston had worked as a front office assistant to Walsh with the 49ers, before leaving to pursue a chance to coach a team in the United States Football League, which was still on the drawing board.

And nobody was more amazed with what Walsh was accomplishing than Ralston.

"Everybody talks about the defense," said Ralston, "but it's the offense that's winning for them. Bill has done things with the offense that nobody thought could be done.

"Number one, he's put in a new game plan every week. We coaches have always thought that you had to drill players over and over before they could do anything, but Bill has run through things two or three times and expected players to do it right in the game.

"And they have. Oh, once in a while you see Joe Montana call a timeout because he's not sure exactly what formation they're supposed to be in, but by and large, they've run the offense as well as anybody could.

"The other thing Bill has done is to anticipate what defense the other team will be in and call the play to beat it.

"For instance he'll anticipate that the defense will be a 'five-under zone.' [Three linebackers and two defensive backs in shallow drops and two safeties playing deep.]

"He'll call for a guard to pull out, as if they're running a screen. The defensive backs see that and stay in tight, and a receiver like Dwight Clark will just slip through that first line of defense and be wide open.

"If the other team comes out in a man-to-man, he'll run picks, and again, a receiver will be open somewhere. I'm just amazed at the way he can anticipate."

This time Walsh's preparation would be for the Giants, who had beaten the Philadelphia Eagles in the wild-card playoff game, and he was planning something quite different from the first time the teams had met.

"I just hope it doesn't rain, because that would take away some of the things we'd like to do," he told me, as he outlined the basics of his game plan.

First the 49ers would try to throw deep early in the game. They hadn't done that against the Giants the first time, nor against other teams very often, and Walsh thought the element of surprise would work in his team's favor. The only concern was at left tackle, because Dan Audick was basically a guard playing tackle, but again, the element of surprise would help.

Second, the 49ers would pass to set up the run. Most teams, fearing the blitzing pressure of rookie New York linebacker Lawrence Taylor, had tried to "establish their running game" against the Giants. That conservatism played into the hands of the Giants, and was no doubt one reason the Giants had won four in a row since losing to the 49ers. Walsh would not make that mistake. "If the weather is decent, we plan to throw on 16 of our first 22 plays," he said.

Third, Taylor would have to be neutralized. "He has to be blocked like a lineman," said Walsh of the 245 pound Taylor. Since Johnny Davis was the only 49er back who could block Taylor on a blitz, the 49ers would try to seal off Taylor by blocking him with a lineman—guard John Ayers.

Defensively, the aim would be to stop running back Rob Carpenter. It had been the acquisition of Carpenter in mid-season that had sparked the Giants' drive to the playoff, and he had been the big factor in the Giants' win over the Eagles. Ironically, the 49ers had talked to Houston about acquiring Carpenter earlier in the year, but Houston's asking price at the time was too high.

"He reminds me a lot of [Mark] Van Eeghen of the Raiders," said Walsh, "but he's better."

The game a couple of days later took place just the way

Walsh had outlined it. His offensive game plan worked to perfection.

As he had said, the 49ers threw 16 passes on the first 22 plays. They passed when the New Yorkers least expected it, seven times on the first 12 first downs, for instance.

Montana threw long from the start. The first two bombs misfired, the first because he slightly underthrew Fred Solomon and the second because Solomon clipped. But eventually, Montana and Solomon connected on a 58-yard touchdown pass, and that kind of threat opened up the Giants' defense for shorter passes.

Taylor was neutralized because the 49ers never made the mistake other teams had of not putting anybody in front of him. "Taylor has been most effective when he's coming in from the split side," pointed out Hank Stram. "When the end is split and there's nobody in front of him, he's got a lot of room to go after the quarterback."

The 49ers often lined somebody up directly opposite Taylor—either Clark or one of the tight ends, Charle Young or Eason Ransom. Other times they had Ayers blocking him, and even if the play went to the other side, Taylor was blocked to keep him from pursuing the play.

As a result of the 49ers' strategy, the Giants were often forced to have Taylor drop back in pass coverage, where he was much less disruptive, instead of blitzing. When he did try to blitz, he was usually blocked. Montana was able to operate without worry about Taylor's harassment.

The other critical factor in the 49ers' offensive success was their ability to force the Giants into misreading plays.

"The 49ers throw so many different things at you," noted Stram, an admitted admirer of Walsh, "that it's really difficult to defense them. They've got different men in motion; they line up differently at times."

Some of the things the 49ers showed the Giants in the first half alone:

—Twice they faked reverses, which set up the real thing at a critical point in the second half.

—Montana faked a run to one side and then hit a quick pass to the other.

—On a play-action fake, Ricky Patton carried out his fake so well that he was tackled—at about the same time Solomon was catching a pass behind the Giant coverage for a touchdown.

—On a third-and-one situation, Walsh called on Earl Cooper, the least likely back to carry on a short-yardage situation, and Cooper slanted off-tackle and to the outside for 20 yards.

—Twice they lined up with two wide receivers in the backfield.

Sometimes the plays worked; sometimes they didn't. But they accomplished Walsh's main purpose: the Giants were constantly off balance. Their great linebackers were confused, often caught thinking pass when the 49ers were running, or vice versa. Forty-Niner receivers were getting wide open in the Giants' secondary. Clark was literally 20 yards away from a defender on one completed pass.

The Giants were so baffled by the 49er offense that the 49ers were able to score 38 points, a total exceeded only by their outburst against Dallas early in the season. In turn, they forced the Giants out of their game plan, which was to control the play with their defense and Carpenter's running. The Giants had to throw twice as often as they ran, and Carpenter was never a factor, with just 61 yards in 17 carries.

The only problem was the 49er defense was giving up points almost as easily, and sometimes more quickly, than the 49er offense was scoring. Suffering an obvious case of playoff nerves, the rookie defensive backs played like...well, like rookies. Mixups on passes that should have been short gains at best resulted in 59-and 72-yard touchdowns, and the Giants' second-year quarterback, Scott Brunner, passed for 290 yards, the most any quarterback had gotten against the 49ers all season.

Scott Brunner?

Once again the 49ers scored first, on an eight-yard pass from Montana to Young in the first quarter, but the Giants tied it up on the first of the bizarre plays by the 49er secondary.

Brunner threw a pass to Earnest Gray that should have been good for 12 yards. Carlton Williamson, in position to tackle Gray, took his eyes off the receiver because he thought the ball would be intercepted. It wasn't, Williamson missed his tackle, Ronnie Lott and Dwight Hicks collided, and Gray went 72 yards for a touchdown.

Then the 49ers hit a hot stretch that should have put the game out of reach. First Ray Wersching hit a 22-yard field goal on the first play of the second quarter. Amos Lawrence had returned the kickoff (following Gray's touchdown) for 47 yards to the New York 45, and Montana had set up the field goal with a 38-yard pass to the wide-open Clark.

Next, Montana hit Solomon on a 58-yard touchdown pass that was the best-executed play of the afternoon. The faking by

Montana and Patton was so good that blitzing linebacker Harry Carson, in position to sack Montana, turned around and tackled Patton instead.

Keena Turner recovered a fumble on the New York 41, and three plays later, Patton raced 25 yards for a touchdown, his second-longest run of the season. Wersching's PAT added to the 49ers comfortable lead, 24-7.

Then Joe Danelo's 40-yard field goal made it 24-10 at the intermission and, though the 49ers had trouble moving the ball in the third quarter and couldn't score at all, they would still have been safely in the lead but for another of those fluke plays in the secondary.

This time it was a gamble by Lott that misfired. Covering Johnny Perkins on a short pass, he was confused by the tight end's move. He tried for an interception and missed, and Perkins went 59 yards for a touchdown. Danelo's PAT made it 24-17.

'Twas a bad time for the 49ers. They had dominated play in the first half, but now their own mistakes had let the Giants back in the game. Given a half to study what the 49ers were doing, the Giants' coaching staff had finally figured a way to defense them, and the 49ers hadn't been able to move the ball with any consistency in the second half. With the Giants only a touchdown back, anything could happen.

Then the game started swinging back to the 49ers. First the erratic Danelo, who had been in a terrible slump for several games, hit the right upright with an attempted 21-yard field goal which would have pulled the Giants to within four points.

Moments later Solomon returned a punt 22 yards, deep into Giants' territory. But the 49ers started moving inexorably backward, not forward, and they faced a third-and-18 situation on the New York 41, well out of field goal range and seemingly unable to move closer.

And then Gary Jeter took a swing at 49er tackle Dan Audick in full view of an official. The resulting penalty gave the 49ers a first down on the New York 26.

"He was holding me," Jeter said later. "The play was over, and he kept pushing me downfield. All linemen hold, but he was holding the entire game."

Solomon went 12 yards on a reverse to the 14, the play that had been set up by faked reverses earlier, and Bill Ring got the final three yards two plays later.

Though both teams would each make another touchdown, for a final score of 38-24, the game was effectively over.

As if to underscore that point, the weather changed

dramatically. Only a light rain had fallen throughout the game, not enough to change the 49ers' plans, but a violent storm was about to hit the Bay Area, dropping as much as 12 inches of rain in 36 hours and devastating areas of Marin, San Mateo, and Santa Clara counties. For the next week, there would be only two significant topics of conversation in much of Northern California: that storm and the 49ers chances against Dallas.

15

THE REAL SUPER BOWL

Dallas. Forget what the NFL schedule said. "This is the *real* Super Bowl," said Lou Spadia, and thousands of long-suffering 49er fans would agree.

Everybody remembered that Dallas had beaten the 49ers in the NFC championship game two years running (1970 and 1971). Everybody remembered the miracle finish in the 1972 playoff game, when Roger Staubach had gotten two touchdowns in less than two minutes to stun the 49ers.

More than that, though, the Cowboys put off people with their arrogance. They were "America's Team," by self-design; one wonders what the vote would have been outside of Texas. When they were beaten, as they had been by the 49ers, it was because "Those weren't the real Cowboys out there today," or "They didn't beat the real Cowboys." What other team could dismiss a 31-point loss so easily?

"I'm tired of hearing that the *real* Cowboys didn't show up," snapped John Brodie. "They said that when we beat them, and they said that when the Giants beat them. How many players do they have on their roster, anyway?"

Though the Cowboys had their share of spectacular players (Tony Dorsett, Danny White, Tony Hill, and Drew Pearson), their image was that of a perfect franchise, and perfection is always boring. They did everything by computer, and computers are never wrong. (Actually, it had originally been the 49ers' proposal to start a scouting combine that utilized computers to organize the information, but the Cowboys' got the credit for it.) If a player didn't meet the Cowboys' physical and mental standards for a particular position, he wasn't drafted. Other teams' tendencies were broken down by the computer. Plays were rated on a percentage basis.

"Dallas has the personality of a video game," sniffed KNBR's Mike Cleary.

The local fans' dislike of the Cowboys was accompanied by apprehension. Dallas seemed to be reaching its peak at exactly the right time. The week before they crushed the Tampa Bay Buccaneers, 38-0. The Cowboys' pass rushers sacked Tampa Bay quarterback Doug Williams four times for 39 yards lost, forced him into four interceptions and two intentional groundings, and held him to ten completions in 29 attempts.

"There's no way anybody could have beaten Dallas today," said Williams. "We didn't have a chance, and I don't know if any other team would have either."

"I guess you could say we were awesome," said Cowboy linebacker D. D. Lewis.

That lopsided win added to the Dallas mystique, as did the contention that the Cowboys were at their best in the playoffs. In fact, at the two highest playoff levels they had lost as many as they had won; they were 5-4 in championship games, 2-3 in the Super Bowl.

Forty-Niner fans were edgy, too, because their team had beaten Dallas, and badly, in the regular season. Traditionally, the Cowboys revenged themselves in the playoffs for losses during the year. In 1980, for instance, the Rams had beaten the Cowboys, 38-14, in the regular season; in the playoffs Dallas smothered them, 34-13.

None of this bothered either the 49er coaches or players; they were confident they could win.

"We think we'll win because we have a better team," said quarterback coach Sam Wyche, a few days before the game. "We're very confident. We might beat them by two touchdowns."

At the press conference for head coaches Bill Walsh and Tom Landry the Friday before the game, one reporter asked Walsh why he would have confidence going into the game.

"I really wanted to tell him, 'Well, we beat them, 45-14. Why shouldn't we?'" said Walsh later. "We felt confident because we had played Dallas before and played very well against them. We had a formula as to what they do in moving the ball; defensively, too, we felt we had a good grasp of how to deal with them. I felt we were a quicker team than they were."

After the game, Wyche and offensive line coach Bobb McKittrick explained the reasons for their optimism.

"Our guys were playing good, and we felt like we could out-play them again," Wyche said. "I really felt good about the way our guys were playing, the way we would pass protect, which we did. I still think they have a good team, but I just thought that our guys were playing at the top of their game. The offense felt good about how we matched up against their defense."

"I felt we ought to get four touchdowns against them at least," McKittrick added. We knew it would be tougher than the first time, but we also knew they were going to line up the same way and that they were going to use basically the same pass coverages. Because of what we felt were weaknesses, we thought we could move the ball on them."

The players felt that confidence from the coaches. "You could hear it in the way they were talking," said Dwight Clark, "and the closer the game got, instead of getting more uptight, Bill and Sam and all the rest of the coaches seemed to get more confident and more loose about the game, like they knew we were better, and they knew we should win."

Walsh, though, made only one public prediction: "It will take four touchdowns to win this game." He was exactly right.

* * * *

It wouldn't have been a 49er game without at least one surprise, and Walsh's surprise came early, when he started Lenvil Elliott at running back.

Elliott started his career in 1973 in Cincinnati when Walsh was still an assistant there. Though never more than a spot player for the Bengals, he'd been a dangerous runner with good speed and an excellent pass receiver.

Released by Cincinnati after the 1978 season, he'd been picked up by the 49ers and had played well for them, again as a spot player. In 1980, he averaged 4.5 yards a carry in gaining 341 yards, and caught 27 passes for 285 yards.

But Elliott was coming off knee surgery, and he was 30 years old, playing a position which few had played beyond age 27 or 28 in the NFL. He had lost most of the speed that had distinguished his early-career play.

He was cut in training camp, when the roster was pared to 50, but that had been a tactical maneuver; Walsh reasoned that other clubs wouldn't pick up a 30-year-old running back, so Elliot would be available later if needed. After the first game of the season, he was re-signed and was active for five games. After a knee injury in mid-October, he was put on injured reserve.

"We kidded him a lot," said Randy Cross. "We told him he was going to sit back on a lake fishing for six or seven weeks. We said, 'We'll call you when the money games come.'"

Elliott went home to Cincinnati and kept himself in shape. Near the end of the season he returned to San Francisco and worked out with the team. When Paul Hofer went on injured reserve with a knee injury, Elliott was activated. Walsh used one of his "moves," so Elliott wouldn't have to pass waivers.

Walsh was starting Elliott because of his experience and his pass catching ability. If fans and writers were surprised, the players weren't. "We knew Lenvil had his legs back," said Hofer, "and we knew he'd do the job. He's very reliable."

* * * *

In pro football, the importance of a game doesn't guarantee excitement. Sometimes players and coaches are so tense and cautious in a big game that teams probe tentatively for weaknesses, trying nothing more daring than an off-tackle run. There's an outstanding example of that in Dallas history: the 1970 playoff game when the Cowboys beat Detroit 5-0. Yawn.

Nobody went to sleep at this game. God, what a game this was! For more than three hours, the 49ers and Cowboys attacked and retreated and attacked once again, the lead changing hands six times. There were spectacular plays, controversial calls, a gut-wrenching drive at the end, and finally, a catch by Dwight Clark that will forever be known as *The Catch* in San Francisco sports history.

The action was nonstop, starting in a first quarter that produced 17 points. The first score came when the 49ers drove 63 yards in eight plays, almost all of it coming on Joe Montana's four-for-five passing, for 60 yards. Montana hit Elliott for 24 yards to the Dallas eight, and then connected with Fred Solomon in the end zone for the touchdown.

Dallas countered with a 44-yard field goal by Rafael Septien, and then got a big break when Mike Hegman recovered a fumble by Bill Ring (caused by a resounding Bob Breunig tackle) on the San Francisco 29. Two plays later Danny White hit Tony Hill for 26 yards and a touchdown.

The 49ers weren't deterred, marching 47 yards in four plays in the second quarter to retake the lead. The drive-concluding touchdown came off of brilliant individual efforts by both Montana and Clark.

Clark put on a couple of moves that left Dallas defensive back Dennis Thurman spinning around and heading in the

(left) Eric Wright intercepts a pass against Pittsburgh and looks for running room. (top right) Walt Easley slips through a tackle, also against Pittsburgh. Johnny Davis protects the ball as he rams for short yardage against Green Bay.

(top left) Forty-Niner fans wait at Candlestick in the wet, cold weather to buy tickets for the NFC championship game. (lower left) Fumble! The ball pops loose in the playoff game against the Giants, and Bobby Leopold is there to make a critical recovery to set up an early score.   On the sidelines, Archie Reese cheers as the clock winds down in the championship game. The 49ers have won, and the Super Bowl is the next stop.

(top left) Randy Cross prepares to block in the NFC championship game. Cross had the best year of his career and made the Pro Bowl game because of his contributions to the 49er season. (bottom left) End of the road! Forty-niner defensive end Jim Stuckey is about to nail Los Angeles running back Wendell Tyler after a short gain. (right) Ray Wersching is deep in contemplation during a Silverdome workout before Super Bowl. Placekicking is all concentration and ritual, and Wersching has several superstitious routines. The most obvious is the fact that he never looks at the goal posts when he comes out for a kick, depending on holder Joe Montana to line him up properly. It all works: Wersching is one of the game's best clutch kickers.

(left) Joe Montana seems to be praying as he stands on the sidelines, but Joe's contributions went far beyond praying during the Super Bowl season. (top right) Charle Young is sent flying by a tackle after catching a pass in playoff game against the Giants. It's a hard way to earn a living. (bottom left) Carlton Williamson is concentrating on the ball as Dallas receiver tries to get there first.

(top left) Dan Audick prepares to make a block in the Atlanta game. Audick, at less than 250 pounds, is really more suited to playing offensive guard, but he filled in at tackle admirably during the season, using his quickness to compensate for lack of bulk. (bottom left) Lawrence Pillers closes in on Green Bay quarterback David Whitehurst, who is trying to run after failing to spot an open reciever. (right) Barefooted punter Jim Miller had his ups-and-downs, but he kicked magnificently in the Super Bowl, outkicking Cincinnati's Pat MacInally, considered the best in the game.

(top left) Keith Fahnhorst shows intense determination as he prepares to make a block. (bottom left) Dwaine Board is just a step away from sacking Los Angeles quarterback Pat Haden. (right) Archie Reese shows why he is such a force in the middle as he swats down a pass from Tampa Bay quarterback Doug Williams. (overleaf) Forty-Niner owner Ed DeBartolo Jr. talks on the phone during a timeout in game. (last page) The 49er cable cars wind their way through the Market Street crowd in victory parade the day after the Super Bowl. An estimated half-million people showed up to cheer the 49ers, and the crowd was so large that the parade route had to be altered; the cable cars could not get through.

DAN AUDICK

JOHN AYERS

GUY BENJAMIN

DWAINE BOARD

DAN BUNZ

JOHN CHOMA

RICKY CHURCHMAN

DWIGHT CLARK

EARL COOPER

RANDY CROSS

JOHNNY DAVIS

FRED DEAN

WALT DOWNING

WALT EASLEY

KEITH FAHNHORST

WILLIE HARPER

JOHN HARTY

DWIGHT HICKS

PAUL HOFER

PETE KUGLER

AMOS LAWRENCE

BOBBY LEOPOLD

RONNIE LOTT

SALADIN MARTIN

MILT McCOLL

JIM MILLER

JOE MONTANA

RICKY PATTON

LAWRENCE PILLERS

CRAIG PUKI

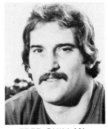

FRED QUILLAN

EASON RAMSON

ARCHIE REESE

JACK REYNOLDS

BILL RING

MIKE SHUMANN

FREDDIE SOLOMON

JIM STUCKEY

LYNN THOMAS

KEENA TURNER

RAY WERSCHING

CARLTON WILLIAMSON

MIKE WILSON

ERIC WRIGHT

CHARLE YOUNG

BILL WALSH

CAS BANASZEK

NORB HECKER

MILT JACKSON

BILLIE MATTHEWS

BOBB McKITTRICK

BILL McPHERSON

RAY RHODES

GEORGE SEIFERT

CHUCK STUDLEY

AL VERMEIL

SAM WYCHE

wrong direction as Clark raced uncovered to the middle of the end zone.

Meanwhile Montana was being doggedly pursued by Too Tall, who finally grabbed the 49er quarterback around the ankles. But just at that moment Montana spotted Clark; as he was going down, Montana lofted a soft pass that Clark gathered in for the score.

The Cowboys came back, with a big assist from the officials. Starting on his own 20, White moved his team to the 37; from there he completed a sideline strike to Tony Hill right in front of the 49er bench at the San Francisco 47.

"He was clearly out of bounds," said Walsh later. "It wasn't even close. He was standing next to me when he caught it."

What followed was even worse, a call by side judge Dean Look that would have been the subject of bitter controversy if it had decided the game, as it appeared it would until the very end.

Then White tried to hit wide receiver Drew Pearson on a long pass down the right sideline. Lott was in perfect position and intercepted the pass, but Look threw his handkerchief and called pass interference, giving the Cowboys a first down at the Niners' 12.

As television replays clearly showed, it was Pearson who was doing the bumping, not Lott. Coming from behind, the Cowboy receiver was climbing all over Lott trying to get to the ball.

Asked for an explanation of his call, Look said that the bumping had occurred upfield when Lott had first moved in front of Pearson. But the flag hadn't been thrown at that point; it was seconds later, when Lott made the interception, that Look called the penalty. And the ball was placed considerably further downfield from where Lott had cut in front of Pearson. Clearly Look had put together his explanation after the fact, probably after he had been told that the replays didn't show interference.

The Cowboys needed no more help after that, and Dorsett got the final five yards easily, sweeping outside for the score that put Dallas up 17-14 at halftime.

Nobody thought anything was decided at that point; now the 49ers had a turn. After Bobby Leopold had intercepted a tipped pass, San Francisco went 13 yards to score in four plays. It wasn't easy. Three plays brought the 49ers just short of the three-yard line. Walsh made his choice: go for the touchdown. The Cowboys were offsides, giving the 49ers a first down on the two, and Johnny Davis scored on the next play. The 49ers had the lead going into the fourth quarter.

Less than a minute into that final quarter, the Cowboys drew to within a point on Septien's 22-yard field goal. Lott was called for another pass interference penalty on the drive, this one a good call. Though it gave the Cowboys a first down on the San Francisco 12, ironically the call may actually have worked in the 49ers' favor. On third down in that series, Eric Wright knocked down a pass in the end zone and the play could have been ruled interference. To this observer, at least, it seemed nobody was going to call a third critical pass interference penalty against the 49ers. In the trade, that's known as "evening out." NFL officials are human, if just barely.

Midway through the period, another critical break occurred as Walt Easley fumbled after a hard Breunig hit, the Cowboys recovering on the 50. It was the sixth turnover for the 49ers (three interceptions and three fumbles), an incredible statistic for a team with only 25 turnovers in 16 regular season games.

The Cowboys covered those 50 yards in just four plays, Doug Cosbie taking White's 21-yard pass for the score. Septien's PAT made it 27-21, Cowboys, with 4:19 gone in the last quarter.

An exchange of punts left the 49ers pinned back on their 11 with less than five minutes remaining. It looked like the end. Nothing had gone right for the 49ers, not with six turnovers and a controversial pass interference call.

Owner DeBartolo had already given up. He was heading down to the dressing room to commiserate with his players. But on the field the coaches and players were still optimistic.

"Almost five minutes left and all our timeouts," Walsh said later. "I liked our chances. If we got as far as the 35, we'd go for it on the fourth down, no matter what."

"We knew, going into that drive, that they hadn't really stopped us yet," Cross said. "We stopped ourselves most of the time. It was so ironic to look up at the scoreboard and see the score, 27-21, because I just knew what the score had to be. I just knew it."

Montana had thrown three interceptions, two of them into coverage, but he wasn't discouraged either. "It was a very confident feeling in the huddle," he said. "We had to move the ball, and we knew we could."

The Cowboys played into the 49ers' hands by going into the notorious "prevent defense," playing six defensive backs. Coaches never learn, even as smart a one as Tom Landry.

The "prevent" works best when the offensive team has little time left and has to throw long; receivers going deep are always double-covered in that formation.

But the 49ers were hardly in that desperate a situation. They had plenty of time and thus, no reason to restrict their offense, which is geared to short- and medium-range passes. Because the Cowboys were playing only three defensive linemen, they wouldn't be able to put much pressure on Montana. A final important point: the "prevent" is vulnerable to runs.

The first play, a swing pass from Montana to Elliott, misfired when Elliott couldn't handle the low throw. The next, a draw to Elliott, went for six yards. "We had to slow their rush down a little bit," said Wyche.

A sideline pass to Solomon gained six yards and gave the 49ers a first down on the 23, and then the 49ers ran some more. First they swept right: Elliott gained 11 yards behind the blocking of Cross and John Ayers. Elliott ran the same play the other way for another seven yards. A Dallas offsides gave the 49ers a first down, and then Montana hit Earl Cooper for a five-yard pass at the two-minute warning.

Cross, who had been battling the flu all day, vomited on the field. "I'd thrown up on the sidelines twice before that," he said. "This time I couldn't make it over there." But there was no way he was going to leave the game.

On the sidelines Walsh and Montana talked about what play to call next, and Walsh decided on a reverse to Solomon. "I thought Dallas was a little tired and might have trouble reacting," Walsh later explained. And he was right: Solomon went for 14 yards on the play.

Then Montana threw a sideline pass to Clark, against double coverage by Dallas corner Eversen Walls and extra back Benny Barnes. Walls had already intercepted two passes, but that didn't faze Montana. This time Walls just tipped the ball but Clark maintained his concentration and grabbed it for a ten-yard gain before going out of bounds.

There was a minute and a half left now. Montana hit Solomon crossing underneath the coverage for 12 yards and a first down on the Dallas 13, and then he called time with 1:15 left.

Cross looked across at the Cowboys and thought they had a beaten look. Probably it was just fatigue. The game had taken its physical and emotional toll on almost everybody.

But nobody seemed in worse shape than Niner Dwight Clark, who had lost seven pounds battling the flu that week. The game doesn't come easy for Clark. Lacking the speed of a receiver like Solomon, he's usually tackled as soon as he gets the ball, and he takes a terrible beating during the course of a game. That had been true again on this day, and he was spent.

The 49ers went for it all on the next play, with Solomon breaking free into the left corner as Mike Wilson helped screen off a defender with his move the other way. But Montana's pass sailed wide. Walsh screamed in frustration.

"I thought that was the championship right there," he said. "We were never going to get that open again. It had worked perfectly to get Solomon free in the end zone, and we missed it."

It was time to run the sweep again, and Elliott ran left for another seven yards. The 49ers took their second timeout, stopping the clock with 58 seconds left. The Cowboys went back to a normal defense, with three linebackers.

Walsh called the play that had given the 49ers their first touchdown and had been a key play all year, one of the first that they had put in during training camp at Rocklin. Solomon was to line up inside Clark on the right side and then cut to the right side of the end zone while Clark was cutting first inside and then back outside. Montana, rolling right, would look for Solomon first and then, if Solomon were covered, for Clark.

The teams lined up, the ball was snapped, and suddenly Too Tall Jones, the Cowboys' huge All-Pro defensive end, was chasing Montana. Solomon was covered; Clark had double coverage in the end zone. Just before Jones could bury him, Montana lofted a pass to the rear of the end zone. Jones thought he was putting the ball up for grabs. Nobody was open. Those watching thought he was just throwing the ball away. But Clark lifted his tired body in a leap that even he thought impossible and caught the ball, coming down just inbounds. The 49ers had tied the game.

A wall of noise came from the stands, a steady blast of sound which didn't abate until long after Ray Wersching had kicked his thirty-sixth consecutive point-after to give the 49ers a 28-27 lead.

In the press box, where writers are often cautioned by announcer Stu Smith to remember "The press box is a working area and no cheering is allowed," there were shrieks of joy and dismay, depending on where the writers were from. Stu Smith be damned; anybody who could have remained calm at that point was a robot, fit only to play for Dallas.

The play meant that Walsh didn't have to spring his last surprise: if the pass had failed, Walsh planned to run a sweep against the tired Cowboys on the fourth down, knowing full well that he'd have to be prepared for an avalanche of criticism if the run failed.

The game was not over yet. The Cowboys still had a chance to move into range for what could have been a winning field goal, and many thought they would do just that when White passed to Pearson for 31 yards to put the Cowboys on the San Francisco 44 with 38 seconds left.

But on the next play, Lawrence Pillers broke through to sack White, who fumbled as he was trying to bring his arm up to pass. Jim Stuckey recovered, and the 49ers were league champions for the first time in their 36-year history.

All week the 49ers said that to win they had to eliminate the mistakes they'd made against the Giants the previous week. They hadn't eliminated those mistakes, but they had still won.

"Six turnovers, and we still won," said Jack Reynolds, forgetting to be a grouch. "I don't know how we did it. With the number of turnovers we made, we should have been blown out. If we didn't make all those mistakes, it wouldn't have been that close."

Cross thought the conclusion was inescapable. "We're the better team," he said, and the statistics backed his contention. The 49ers made 26 first downs, a season high, and gained 393 yards; Dallas had 16 first downs and 250 yards.

But Landry wasn't convinced. "I don't think the 49ers are a better team," he said. "Sometimes in a game like this, it just depends on who has the ball last."

His players were in a somber mood, most of them just sitting on their stools in shock. "We all had visions of a winning field goal," said linebacker D. D. Lewis. "I was thinking of a lot of times we came back to win. We just came up one play short of getting into the Super Bowl. It's a blow, but I'm not about to hang my head down and be sorry."

"It was frustrating to sit on the sideline and watch the last 49er drive," said quarterback White, "but that's the way great games end up. I felt like going out on the field and trying to tackle somebody.

"You can't really say where we lost it. It was a matter of two great teams going at it. It's times like this that we earn our money. People think we're overpaid, but believe me, it's not any fun. No amount of money in the work would make me feel better.

"I learned you've got to play 60 minutes and take advantage of every opportunity. It's going to be a long time before we can do that again. This is one of those games you never get over."

In the 49er dressing room, Fahnhorst was remembering his pre-game nerves. "Joe had to talk to me. He'd won a national championship in college, so this was no big thing to him. I'd never won any damn thing. He calmed me down."

Archie Reese spoke quietly about his feeling of confidence. "It never came into my mind that we were going to lose," he said. "We overcame adversity because we played our hearts out, and we're going to need that to get ready for the Super Bowl."

But, as usual, it was the articulate Cross who best summed it up. "I knew we would win because I read it in my horoscope," he said, pointing to the neatly-folded newspaper in his locker.

His horoscope: "You feel positive and highly revved-up about a dream you've been pursuing."

16

A WORLD CHAMPIONSHIP

When the 49ers arrived by bus at their hotel in the Detroit suburbs the Sunday before the Super Bowl, they were greeted by a white-haired man in a bellman's cap and uniform.

"Help you with your bag, sir? Help you with your bag?" the man repeated to several of the players. It was several moments before the players recognized the "bellhop" in the darkness.

It was Bill Walsh.

Walsh had left San Francisco on Saturday morning, the day before the players left on their United DC-10 charter with "49er Liner" painted on the side; he was scheduled to appear at a Touchdown Club banquet in Washington, D.C., where he was honored as Coach of the Year. From there he'd flown to Detroit early Sunday, arriving before his team.

The sidewalk scene was a reminder of Walsh's love of a practical joke. The players had learned that much earlier, in the exhibition season. He'd sternly informed them before the first road game that he expected them to wear coats and ties on the plane because they were representing San Francisco. *He* showed up for that trip dressed in a general's uniform, while his assistants were dressed in jeans. For the rest of the season's road trips, the players dressed...shall we say extremely casually?

The bellman routine was also Walsh's way of letting the players know they could have a good time during Super Bowl week. It didn't have to be a grim experience, as it had been for some teams.

The Super Bowl is unique in American sports. There are other big events—the World Series, the Kentucky Derby, the Indianapolis 500—but none match the Super Bowl as a spectacle, nor do they equal the attention riveted on it by media and fans.

The World Series, the closest comparison one can make to the Super Bowl, is played in October when the pro and college football seasons are in full swing and pro basketball is about to start. As much attention as the World Series gets, there's still big competition for space on the sports pages.

The Super Bowl, in contrast, is played at a slow moment in the sports year. The only significant competition for attention comes from basketball and hockey, and neither comes close to having the broad base of fan interest of football and baseball.

The big game is played in late January, when everybody needs a pickup. The excitement of the holiday season is past, the weather ranges from bad to terrible throughout the country, and everyone is looking for some excitement. (The Super Bowl doesn't always provide a lot of excitement, but that's another story.)

It's a television game, much more so than the World Series, or any event other than a championship fight. Baseball has never televised well because its action is so spread out; split camera work helps, but it doesn't capture the essence of the game. Football televises beautifully; multiple cameras and instant replays often make the game seem more exciting at home than it is at the stadium. The time between plays is perfect for the use of replays and sometimes informative comments by the color commentators.

The media blitz during Super Bowl week is incredible. This year it would be even worse because the game was being played in snow- and ice-bound Pontiac (possibly the worst decision for a site since the 1980 Olympics were scheduled for Moscow); there would be no idle distractions for writers. "Nobody will be playing golf," observed Walsh.

The same stories would be written over and over; the same questions would be asked over and over, until athletes' minds were numb. There's some respite for team members during the World Series because games are played almost every day, so new plays and new decisions can always be asked about. During Super Bowl week everything leads up to a single game, and there are no new questions to ask. The players hate it, but having been on the other side many times, I can tell you that the writers hate it just as much.

How all this attention is handled can make a big difference to a team. The problem isn't so much the star players, more accustomed to a lot of attention, but the lesser players, who are not. During this particular week, a reserve offensive lineman named Allen Kennedy, who had hardly played all season for the 49ers, found that even he was being interviewed.

Some coaches had handled the media blitz effectively. When coaching the Oakland Raiders, John Madden simply included player interviews and press conferences as part of the daily schedule, not letting the players think of them as anything added. "I told them there were just certain things we had to do, so they might as well enjoy them. I always felt something couldn't be distracting as long as you knew about it."

Pittsburgh coach Chuck Noll seemed to take everything in stride too, though he drove the writers crazy because they could never understand the point of his stories. (Noll has a sense of humor so dry that only one other person in the world understands it, and that person hasn't been found yet.)

But some coaches did have trouble dealing with the attention. George Allen resented it, feeling that it took time away from his preparation. Bud Grant reinforced his image as a cold, emotionless man (an image which is quite distorted, incidentally, as anybody who has dealt with Grant in less frenetic circumstances knows), because he just could not deal with huge press conferences.

It's probably not a coincidence that Madden and Noll were Super Bowl winners and Allen and Grant were losers.

The media blitz started for the 49ers before they even left home, and not just in the sports section. Interviews, including one with Walsh's vivacious wife, Geri, appeared in the society columns; business writers were busy finding aspects of the 49er operation that they could write about. Walsh's customary Tuesday press conference even had to be moved out of the 49er offices to an adjoining building because so many media people showed up.

At that press conference the 49er coach was angered because his team would have to practice early in the morning. Since teams couldn't practice outdoors, they both had to schedule practices in the Silverdome; besides that, the television crews had to have time to work out their complex procedures.

A flip of the coin determined practice times and the 49ers lost; they would have to start practice at 9 a.m. and, worse, hold a press conference an hour earlier. Walsh was especially upset because the NFL had denied his alternative: practicing at the University of Michigan's indoor facilities in Ann Arbor. NFL executive director Don Weiss had told Walsh that the League had been through all this many times and they knew all the factors that had to be taken into account.

"Well, they didn't take into account the fact that one team is traveling across three time zones to the game and the other will be staying in the same time zone," said Walsh. "We'll be talking to the press at 5 o'clock by our body clocks."

The NFL decision on the press conference time was baffling even to writers, who would have much preferred a later hour, both because they would get more information after a practice and because they would be able to sleep later, not necessarily in that order of importance.

Possibly Walsh's anger was more tactical than real, a chance to persuade his players they were really the underdogs, despite the odds posting them as one-to-three-point favorites. He surely realized that the early practices would help the 49ers acclimate to the time change that much faster.

Walsh seemed even more relaxed than he'd been at the start of the season. "I can see the end in sight now," he said. "When you get to the end of the season, you don't have to be as guarded in your statements."

His press conference had run over an hour and a half longer than usual, because groups of reporters came up to talk to him after the formal part had ended. He still had an interview to do with Don Klein of radio station KCBS, but he seemed in no hurry to break away.

"It means that I'll have to stay later tonight to work on my game plan," he told me, "but you just have to accept that as part of the job. You don't want to let that force you to cut your work short. I can't let myself leave early without getting everything done. And I can't worry about it. Some coaches try to turn off the questions so they can get back to their work, but that only gets them more tense. If I have to stay five minutes longer at a press conference, I'll stay five minutes longer."

Walsh planned to do the bulk of his work before the end of the week, right there in Redwood City. "I'm sure we'll have the game plan in by the end of the week," he said. "We can't depend on getting a lot done back there, so we'll have to do it here. And, after all, this is what we usually have to prepare for a game — one week."

He didn't anticipate any special problems in preparing for the Bengals. "I don't mean that it will be easy to stop them," he said, "because they have a lot of weapons, but I don't expect any real surprises from them."

Walsh's approach, as well as his mind, seemed to give the 49ers an edge over the Bengals.

Everybody who wrote or talked of Cincinnati coach Forrest Gregg stressed the "discipline" that Gregg had instilled, and the way he ran a "tight ship." What they meant was that Gregg told the Bengals exactly what to do; the Bengals were not expected to act or think for themselves. That approach can work well during the regular season, but players who depend on it have a tendency to fall apart in unusual situations, a category which succinctly describes the Super Bowl.

Just such a collapse happened to the Philadelphia Eagles in the 1981 Super Bowl. They came into the game as tightly strung as Bjorn Borg's rackets; the relaxed and confident Raiders took them apart.

The 49ers were nearly as loose as the Raiders had been the previous year. "I'm not a drill sergeant," said Walsh. "Players know what they have to do, but I'm not hammering at them all the time.

"I really said nothing to get them up for Dallas. That sort of thing has to come from the players, and we're fortunate to have players like Charle Young who can inspire others. That's really why the Raiders won last year; they had a few players who could get everybody else up."

* * * *

In Detroit, CBS executives were grumbling because two obscure teams had made it to the Super Bowl. They would have preferred big-name teams, like the Cowboys and Steelers, or teams from the two big media centers, New York and Los Angeles.

Still, the 49ers were starting to become known as individuals. Joe Montana was the subject of a cover story in *Time*, and he shared the *Newsweek* cover with Cincinnati's Ken Anderson.

Dwight Clark, too, was frequently interviewed, partially because his girlfriend, Shawn Weatherly, had been Miss Universe. Though they both looked as if they came straight off a Southern California beach, they'd met while attending Clemson in South Carolina.

Perhaps the most interesting 49er, though, was right guard Randy Cross, who was showing up on most of the All-Pro selections. Offensive linemen tend to be conservative men, neat and orderly, accustomed to doing their job with little recognition. Most offensive linemen get noticed only for negative actions, such as penalties or missed blocks that result in quarterback sacks. Cross admitted he was no exception.

"I have very strong feelings about law and order," he said. "But I also have a strong interest in kids, particularly the underprivileged. They're the most helpless, along with the older people. There's nothing they can do for themselves, so there's got to be something done for them."

Off the field, Cross was a gentle, smiling giant of a man who preferred to talk and think about something besides football. His nature didn't change dramatically on the field.

"It's not a personal vendetta out there," he said. "I'm not interested in letting blood. Football is just something I do, and I happen to do it very well. They aren't paying us to get hurt. Our business is to play."

He seemed to have an excellent perspective on the Super Bowl. "I would hate to look back when I'm 77 and say that something in sports was the highlight of my life."

His teammates, too, seemed to be taking the game in stride. Clark, writing a daily "diary" for the *Chronicle*, was frequently kidded. "One night, they told me we had a team meeting — and no press. I said, 'OK, I'll leave my note pad at home.' Randy Cross told me I had to bring my press pass to get into the meeting. One of our public relations people made up a Pro Football Writers card for me. I don't mind the kidding. It's just part of keeping everything loose."

The difference between Walsh's and Gregg's approach was interesting. Gregg had an 11 p.m. curfew; Walsh's curfew was 1 a.m. Walsh allowed the married players to have their wives with them; Gregg didn't. Walsh even let his squad go to a Diana Ross concert on the Friday night before the game.

And when tables were set up to interview players at their hotels, the 49er tables had the players' names on them, while the Cincinnati tables only listed players' numbers.

Walsh was using every possible psychological ploy, starting with an "us against them" mentality because of the treatment the 49ers had gotten from the NFL (worse hotel than the Bengals, bad practice time, etc.).

When Fred Solomon was hurt in a practice collision with Ronnie Lott, Walsh allowed everyone to think the injury was serious by listing the receiver as "questionable" in the NFL injury reports, which means only a fifty-fifty chance of playing.

Solomon got an unusual treatment for his injury, a process perhaps best described as electronic acupuncture. Herb Berger, a salesman who's also a specialist in the field, treated Solomon. Berger is retained by the 49ers. "The 49ers are the only team in the NFL to use this method to speed up the healing process," he said.

He used a rectangular instrument which poked into Solomon's body much as an acupuncturist would put in needles, but Berger was cautious about calling it electronic acupuncture. "It's an electronic physical therapy instrument that incorporates certain acupuncture techniques," he said.

By any name, the treatment apparently worked. Solomon was listed as "probable" the next day, which meant he had an 80 percent chance of playing.

For all the talk about psychology, however, when looking back dispassionately at Super Bowl results, the better team had usually won. Only the New York Jets win in the third Super Bowl was still a real shocker in retrospect, and actually the Jets were a much better team than most people had ever realized.

Games that had seemed a surprise at the time — Kansas City's win over Minnesota, Pittsburgh's win in the Steelers' first Super Bowl appearance against Minnesota — weren't at all, in retrospect. Kansas City and Pittsburgh were clearly better teams.

So, who was the better team in this game? That proposition was debated endlessly. Hank Stram picked the Bengals. Sam Rutigliano, whose Cleveland team had beaten both the Super Bowl teams, thought the 49ers had an edge. I called Sid Gillman, living in retirement near San Diego, and asked his opinion.

Gillman, an assistant for the Eagles the year before, is the acknowledged master of the passing game. Everybody has borrowed from him, from Al Davis to Bill Walsh, though Gillman disagrees with Walsh's high percentage game; Sid prefers the bomb. "I used to kid Bill when he threw all those five-yard passes," said Gillman, "and ask him when he was going to lengthen out to ten yards."

Listening to Gillman is like attending a seminar on the passing game. Predictably, he thought passing would decide this game. "You're never going to see a big game decided by running," he said. "Our game has just changed so much.

"Usually, teams come out conservative because coaches are afraid to make a mistake—no matter what they say the week before. But I don't think that's going to happen this time.

"I know Bill: he'll come out throwing. If he's got 20 plays drawn up, probably 16 of them are passes. And I keep remembering the AFC championship game when Anderson came out in the second quarter and took Cincinnati downfield on practically nothing but passes. If they passed in that weather, God almighty, what will they do inside?"

So, who did he like? "What are the odds?" he asked. Told they were 2–3 points favoring the 49ers, he said, "That would be enough to swing me to Cincinnati if I were betting the game."

Elsewhere, writers were playing the match-up game, rating individual players and positions. Usually the Bengals came out ahead; they had faster receivers, better running backs, bigger offensive linemen. Only in the defensive secondary did the 49ers rate a clear edge.

But these "experts" were missing the point: football is a team game, not a collection of individual efforts, and a team's success depends on how well the individual players mesh. The 49ers always seemed to get the job done. Sometimes their offense fell off and the defense had to win a game; sometimes the defense had slipped and the offense had to play a great game. Whatever it took, the 49ers had had it for 14 of their last 15 games.

Their seeming weaknesses hadn't hurt them. Supposedly the Cincinnati running game was much better, for instance, but the Bengals had averaged only two yards more a game, though playing their home games on artificial turf, while the 49ers were playing in the Candlestick swamp.

And the 49ers were a much more difficult team to prepare for than the Bengals, because of Walsh's intricate game plans.

"We study their game films at least three times more than we do anyone else," said Atlanta defensive coordinator Jerry Glanville. "We thought they were running the best offense even before they were winning. We beat them a couple of times because they weren't very good then, but we were defending them wrong."

Glanville said the 49ers were difficult to defend against because their pass routes were so variable, and he thought it was essential to play zone defense instead of man-to-man (as the Cowboys had done) because the 49er patterns created such confusion in the defensive secondary. The 49ers' ability to cross receivers and screen (pick) defensive backs was especially important, he felt.

"Then somebody's wide open," said Glanville. "I can remember when they played the Jets two years ago. There wasn't anybody near the 49ers' receivers who could hit them with a rock. I love their offense. I love studying it and watching it."

* * * *

The day of the Super Bowl didn't start auspiciously for the 49ers; the bus carrying Walsh and half the team got stuck in traffic. The trip from the 49ers' hotel to the Silverdome was supposed to take 25 minutes, but instead took an hour and ten minutes. The team was expected to be on the field for warmups at 3:05, and those players who had come to the stadium in taxis were becoming somewhat concerned by 2:30.

Walsh was concerned, too, but he was determined not to show it, kidding with his players on the bus.

"I've never in my life been in that situation," he said, "where you're in traffic bumper-to-bumper, police can't clear out the cars, you can't see the stadium, and you're supposed to be on the field in 30 minutes. It takes the players 25 minutes to dress.

"I thought of telling everyone to get off and hold on to each other's arms, and maybe we could ski cross-country."

When the 49ers finally reached the stadium, at 2:40, Walsh was still loose — or pretending to be. "When he walked into the locker room," said Dwight Clark, "he was laughing and joking — like, did we think we were going to have to go without him? He wanted to know who was trying to take over."

Before the game the 49ers played the Kenny Loggins record "This Is It," at the suggestion of Joe Montana. "The song has a message," said Randy Cross. "You have a once-in-a-life-time chance and, as the song says, 'This is your miracle.' You have to grab it."

The players listened to the song once and turned it off, thinking it was time to be serious about the game. Walsh came into the room and said, "Where's the music? Play that song again."

Walsh's approach paid off once the game began. The 49ers were relaxed and confident. Had they not been, they could have been undone by the very first play of the game, when Amos Lawrence fumbled while returning the opening kickoff, with the Bengals recovering on the San Francisco 26.

Ken Anderson went right to work, passing to Isaac Curtis for eight yards, running Pete Johnson up the middle for two, and throwing a quick strike to Dan Ross for 11 yards and a first down on the San Francisco five.

And then the 49ers' defense stiffened. Charles Alexander was stopped for no gain, and Jim Stuckey sacked Anderson for a six-yard loss. On third down Anderson looked for Curtis again, coming across the middle. Dwight Hicks had been helping double-cover Steve Kreider, but when Kreider broke to the out-side, Hicks stayed in the middle. "I don't think Anderson saw me," he said.

As Anderson released the ball, Hicks stepped in front of Curtis and picked off the pass, returning it to the San Francisco 32. The air began to leak out of the Cincinnati balloon right there.

Just as Sid Gillman had predicted, both teams came out throwing. Montana threw on five of the first six 49er plays; with the Bengals looking for the pass, Joe went to the run. The Niners' first Super Bowl touchdown came at the end of a 68-yard drive with a quarterback sneak for the final yard.

That touchdown was significant on a couple of counts. It was the fifteenth time during the season that the 49ers had scored first; in the first fourteen such games their record was 13-1. The team that had scored first had also won thirteen of the previous fifteen Super Bowls.

Once again the 49ers had scored first because a Walsh strategem had confused the opposing defense. This time it was an unbalanced line, added to the game plan only the day before. "The 49ers caught the Bengals in the wrong defense a lot," noted Jack Faulkner, assistant general manager of the Los Angeles Rams and a former coach.

The 49er defense was bothering the Bengals, too. The 49er's used several different defensive formations, including one in which Fred Dean was lined up as a "rover," a linebacker free to move where the ball goes. The 49ers were also waiting until the last possible moment to shift into the defense they would use on a particular play; Jack (Hacksaw) Reynolds was barking defen-sive signals even as Ken Anderson was calling offensive signals for the Bengals.

Cincinnati turned the ball over again early in the second quarter, and again, the 49ers took quick advantage of the mis-cue. It began this way: a Pat McInally punt that got a great Cin-cinnati roll on the carpet backed the 49ers up to their own ten, and Jim Miller had to punt out of the end zone, after the 49ers had advanced only to the 12. His punt went to the Cincinnati 44 and was returned five yards.

Anderson marched his team down to the San Francisco 27. On second down he hit Chris Collinsworth at the five, but when Eric Wright tackled Collinsworth the ball popped loose, and Lynn Thomas recovered for the 49ers at the San Francisco eight.

Once again, though, the 49ers were deep in their own terri-tory. Usually teams are hesitant to throw the ball in this situation because an interception would be so costly. The 49ers ran on the first two plays, Johnny Davis getting just a yard and Bill Ring two yards. But the beauty of Walsh's offense is that it is geared to use the pass as a means of *controlling* the ball. Run properly, it's a low-risk offense, with options available to the quarterback on every play. That means that Montana can throw in virtually any situation ... including this one. On third down he rolled to his right and hit Fred Solomon for 20 yards and a first down. The 49ers were back in business.

In any system, it's important for a coach and quarterback to think alike; in Walsh's system, it's an indispensable attribute. In Montana, Walsh had a quarterback who saw the game as he did, an on-field extension of the coach's thinking.

Probably Walsh had realized that Montana could be this kind of quarterback for him from the start. He had taken great pains with Joe, making sure that the moment was right to use him. Though Steve DeBerg was the starting quarterback during Montana's first two pro years, Walsh would use Montana in situations where he could look good, down near the other team's goal line, so Montana could build up his confidence.

Walsh had never been enthusiastic about DeBerg because DeBerg wasn't mobile enough to escape the rush and couldn't get away from a tendency to throw high-risk passes — which usually resulted in critical interceptions. "I'd hate to think of my reputation depending on Steve DeBerg," he had told me at one point early in the 1980 season.

For a time in 1980, he seemed to waver between DeBerg and Montana, using first one and then the other. That created tension because the two quarterbacks were good friends off the field, and led some writers to think Walsh was being indecisive.

In fact, though, he knew exactly what he was doing. He knew Montana would be his quarterback, but he didn't want Joe playing before he was ready. He didn't want the fans booing Montana for mistakes caused by inexperience, or because his teammates weren't yet good enough.

DeBerg was left in long enough to get the boos; when Montana took over, the fans (and writers) were so happy to see a change made that Montana had a grace period. By the time the honeymoon was over, the 49ers were winning. Montana has never been booed by the home fans, and he may be the only NFL starting quarterback with that distinction.

Now Joe was moving his team downfield again, making the big play when he had to. Chased out of the pocket, he ran for eight yards on one play. Under pressure again, on third down at the Cincinnati 43, he rolled right and tossed one to Clark for 12 yards and a first down.

On first down from the Cincinnati 19, the 49ers ran a reverse with Dwight Clark and got a big break. Clark got hit in the backfield for a two-yard loss ("I tried to put on a move to get away, but I don't have many moves," he said), but Cincinnati linebacker Jim LeClair was called for a late hit. That moved the ball to the Cincinnati 11, where the 49ers had a first down. Television replays showed that LeClair was blocked into Clark and shouldn't have been penalized. The zebras strike again.

On the next play Montana rolled to his right and then looked across the field. Earl Cooper had run to the middle of the field and then cut to his left, and he was open for Montana's pass at the four, bulling his way into the end zone from there. Ray Wersching's kick made it 14-0 and the 49ers were rolling.

With just over four minutes to go in the first half, the 49ers went on the move again. Working the clock down so Cincinnati wouldn't have time to score, the 49ers hustled to the Bengals' five before faltering. Wersching kicked a 22-yard field goal to run the score to 17-0 with just 15 seconds remaining in the half.

All week long Wersching had been practicing squib kicks in the Silverdome. The practice paid off. His kickoffs had skittered along the carpet, taking erratic bounces, and the Bengals had had trouble handling every one. This time, Archie Griffin fumbled Wersching's kick, and the 49ers' Milt McColl recovered on the Cincinnati four.

Only two seconds remained in the half, enough time for Wersching to kick a 26-yard field goal (after the 49ers had been penalized back to the nine for illegal procedure).

The 49ers took a 20-0 lead into their dressing room, the biggest halftime lead any team had ever enjoyed in the Super Bowl. Assistant coach Sam Wyche wrote on the dressing room blackboard, "This game is not over yet." His words became almost frighteningly prophetic in the second half.

The Bengals came out smoking, eager to atone for their first-half mistakes, and the 49ers played like a team that was already counting the winner's share.

"We played the third quarter like everyone thought we would play all year long," said Jim Stuckey. "I think we lost our discipline in the third quarter."

Cincinnati took the opening kickoff, not fumbling this time, and drove 83 yards for its first touchdown — and the first touchdown for the Bengals against the 49ers, who had held them to a field goal in the regular season confrontation.

Only twice did the Bengals have to convert a third down on the drive. On the first one, third-and-four from the Cincinatti 41, Anderson passed to Kreider for 19 yards.

The second time was also third-and-four, on the San Francisco five. Anderson had faded to pass but saw that nobody was coming in from the right side of the 49er defense. He tucked the ball under his arm and ran across for the touchdown. Jim Breech's PAT made it 20-7.

The 49ers ran three plays and punted after their first possession, as they would do the first three times they had the ball in the second half. Now the Bengals had excellent field position, at the San Francisco 49. But the Niners' defense stopped them and forced a punt.

Once again, though, the 49ers went three downs and punted, and this time, the Bengals were ready to move. The big play came on third-and-23 from the Cincinnati 37, when Anderson zeroed in on his outstanding rookie receiver, Collinsworth, for a 49-yard gain to the San Francisco 14.

Three plays later, the Bengals had a first-and-goal at the San Francisco three, and the dramatic sequence that followed probably decided the game.

On first down John Choma stopped Pete Johnson after a two-yard gain, but the Bengals had three downs to make just one yard. "When you're that close," said Cincinnati guard Max Montoya, "if you've got any pride at all, you've got to get it in."

But the Bengals didn't.

On second down Anderson called an audible to change blocking assignments. Wide receiver David Verser was supposed to block a linebacker, but Verser didn't hear the signals because of the crowd noise. He didn't block anybody, and linebackers Reynolds and Dan Bunz stopped Johnson cold for no gain.

On third down Cincinnati offensive coordinator Lindy Infante, who calls all the Bengals' plays, gambled, calling for Anderson to throw to running back Charles Alexander, who was supposed to be just inside the end zone.

Alexander wasn't quite in the end zone when he caught the ball. "I thought I could run in," he said. But Bunz had come up quickly and made a jarring open-field tackle that stopped Alexander in his tracks, perhaps six inches from the goal line.

Everybody knew what was coming next. The Bengals' Johnson, listed at 249 pounds but probably more, and bigger than anybody besides Archie Reese on the 49ers' defensive line, would be carrying the ball. The only question was which direction.

Normally Johnson would have gone left, behind massive tackle Anthony Munoz, but the Bengals thought that might be too obvious. "We had just gone to the left," said Infante. "The decision was, instead, to run the same play, but to turn it around and run it to the other side."

Reynolds had it figured the same way. "The backfield was set up that way," he later said.

Johnson headed into the line, the human bowling ball led into the hole by Alexander, who was supposed to block. "I knocked Alexander back into Pete, and there was nowhere for him to go," said Bunz, who lost his chinstrap and broke the clamp on his helmet. The entire 49er defensive line, and linebackers Bunz and Reynolds, collapsed on Johnson, who fell just short of the goal line. Turned on his back on top of the pile, Reese squirmed and kicked with joy, and the Silverdome rocked with noise. The 49ers had held!

That goal-line stand should have been the clincher, but give the Bengals credit: they didn't concede. After the third straight three-downs-and-punt situation for the 49ers, Cincinnati was on the move again. From the Cincinnati 47, the Bengals moved down to the San Francisco four, helped by a pass interference call against Ronnie Lott.

From the four, Anderson hit tight end Dan Ross for a Bengal touchdown. It was one of eleven passes Ross would catch for a Super Bowl record, and the first of two touchdown passes, tying another Super Bowl mark.

Breech's point-after kick made it 20-14, and the 49ers seemed in serious trouble. The momentum was all with Cincinnatti and there was plenty of time left, more than ten minutes. The 49ers hadn't yet had a first down in the second half; the Bengals had had nine. In the first half, the 49ers had outgained the Bengals, 202-99. In the second half, the Bengals would roll up 257 yards to just 73 for the 49ers.

But all year long the 49ers had been able to make that one drive they had to make to win a game. On the sidelines, they knew what had to be done. "I don't think there was ever a moment of doubt," said offensive tackle Keith Fahnhorst, "but I was getting a little nervous. We had to cool them off and get something, get some momentum going."

In the huddle, one player said, "Think of it as the last ten minutes of your life and you've got to give it everything." Somebody else mentioned the difference between the winning and losing shares, but, as Clark said later, "Money is not the big motivator in this type of situation. No one will ever take away a world championship from me."

The drive didn't start auspiciously. Montana's pass was incomplete on first down, and offensive tackle Dan Audick was penalized for a false start on the next play. It was second-and-15 from the San Francisco 22, and you wouldn't have found many bettors eager to take the 10ers at that point.

Then Walsh called a play that had just been put in for this game. "I was supposed to make them think I was going long," said wide receiver Mike Wilson, one of the 49ers' 15 free agents. "I ran 25 yards down and then came back."

Montana dropped straight back as if he were going to throw deep, and then rolled to his right. On the move, he fired to Wilson on the right sideline, just in front of the Cincinnati bench, at the 44. Cincinnati coach Forrest Gregg and his players jumped up in rage when the official signaled a catch; they were certain Wilson was out of bounds.

That was the play the 49ers needed. Now Walsh could think of both the score and the time. He determined to run some time off the clock, and the 49ers went to a running offense. Montana threw on the first play after Wilson's catch, an incomplete pass; but Cincinnati's Ken Riley was called for pass interference and that gave the 49ers another first down. After that, the 49ers did nothing but run. They knew they had only to get a field goal to put the game effectively out of reach of the Bengals.

Finally, at fourth-and-five on the Cincinnati 23, it was time to call on Wersching, as reliable a kicker as any in the NFL. Wersching went through his usual superstitious routine. He resolutely refuses to look at his target, putting his hand on Montana's shoulder, and looking like a blind man, relying on Joe to line him up correctly.

There was no sloppy turf to worry Wersching this time. There were no variable wind currents in the covered Silverdome. Just the kick.

The snap from Randy Cross came back perfectly. Montana spotted the ball. Wersching kicked it. The ball sailed true through the goal posts, and the 49ers had a 23-14 lead.

The 49ers had run the clock down to just over five minutes, and Cincinnati's position was precarious indeed. The Bengals now needed both a touchdown and a field goal.

The Bengals were soon in an even deeper hole. On their first play from scrimmage after the kickoff, Anderson tried to hit Collinsworth but Wright stepped in front of the Bengal receiver at the Cincinnati 47 and ran the ball back 25 yards. For one fleeting moment, Wright almost gave it back. As he was tackled, he tried to lateral to linebacker Willie Harper, but he couldn't control the flip and the ball bounced loose on the carpet. But Harper finally recovered it for the 49ers.

Now more than ever it was important for the 49ers to run time off the clock and force Cincinnati to use its timeouts. Three running plays gained a first down. Two more resulted in a net loss of three yards. On third down Montana rolled left and gained seven — and he stayed in bounds so the clock wouldn't stop.

Close enough. On the fourth down Wersching came in to kick his fourth field goal, tying a Super Bowl record, from 23 yards out. 49ers, 26-14.

The Bengals got the ball back, starting on their own 26 after the kickoff, with no timeouts left. Anderson took his team smartly downfield to score in just six plays, the last one a three-yard pass to Ross for the touchdown. But surprisingly, Anderson didn't throw any passes to the sidelines to stop the clock; all his passes were into the middle of the field. That meant that the clock never stopped, and only 16 seconds remained when Cincinnati scored to make it 26-21.

On the kickoff the Bengals went for an onsides attempt, but Clark smothered the ball before any Cincinnati player could get to it. The 49ers ran one play, Montana falling on the ball, and Superbowl XVI was all over.

* * * *

In the 49er dressing room NFL commissioner Pete Rozelle, presenting the Vince Lombardi trophy to owner Edward DeBartolo, Jr., and Walsh, noted that, "This is the greatest turnaround in Super Bowl history, from 6-10 to Super Bowl champions."

Walsh took a phone call from President Reagan, whom he had met while in Washington to accept the Coach of the Year trophy from the Touchdown Club, and then told the press that the Super Bowl win was the "highlight of my life."

"This is a group of men who do not have great talent," he said, "but they have great inspiration. No one could take us this year."

The players showed their reaction in different ways. "We're world champs!" Lynn Thomas screamed across the room at Ronnie Lott. Keith Fahnhorst wondered, "What can we ever do to top this?"

The usually whimsical Charle Young was serious, perhaps for the first time. Young loves to put on writers, and turn interviews around so that he is the one asking questions. The first time we had met, he had told me that, judging from the way I was dressed, I should be a college professor who drove a Volvo. (I will never be a professor, but he was right about the second part of the equation.) When I wrote this year that the 49ers needed a tight end who could get deep, he came up to me in the dressing room the next week and thanked me for writing that. "It made me play harder," he said.

This time, though, there were no jokes, no put-ons. "I came from the basement, from not being able to play, to this," he said in wonderment.

Finally, Hacksaw Reynolds forgot for the moment that he is supposed to be the team's resident grouch. The man who had talked all year of the team's "luck" and doubted before each game that the 49ers could win, said, "We were obviously good, possibly great, and nobody can take that away from us."

Amen.

POSTSCRIPT

San Francisco has a reputation as a sophisticated city, but the reaction to the 49ers' Super Bowl win, during the game and after, certainly belied that.

The game itself smashed all records for television watching, with almost 2.6 million Bay Area TV sets tuned in to the game. "We claim with total confidence that the game had the biggest Bay Area audience ever for any program, sports or otherwise," said Andrea Hine of KPIX-TV, San Francisco's CBS outlet.

The ratings jumped as high as 55.7, with a 93 share during the critical third quarter. That meant that 55.7 percent of all the sets in the Bay Area were tuned to the game, and 93 percent of the sets in use were on the game. By comparison, the 1981 Super Bowl, in which the Oakland Raiders beat the Philadelphia Eagles, had a 50.7 rating and 82 share.

The telecast surpassed the two previous record holders, the 49ers' championship win over Dallas and the final installment of the serial "Roots."

Newspapers also benefited from the great interest. The *San Francisco Chronicle,* which has the largest circulation of any Bay Area newspaper, sold about 100,000 more copies than usual; the 625,000 copies sold represented the largest one-day sale in *Chronicle* history.

In the aftermath of the game, San Francisco became the scene of one continuous party. Traffic came to a stop in many parts of town, and areas such as North Beach, Union Square, and Union Street were closed off because huge crowds were milling in the streets. It was a scene reminiscent of the celebrations following the end of World War II, as people kissed and hugged total strangers.

As the celebrants drank more and more, the scene turned rough. Eventually there were 83 arrests, 125 people treated and released at city hospitals, and four police officers injured.

"It was not a riot," said a police spokesman, Sergeant Michael Pera, "but it was violent for a short time in some places."

The wildest scene was yet to come. The next day, after the 49ers returned home on their chartered plane, the city held a victory parade and virtually everybody came.

A tremendous throng overflowed Civic Center Plaza as the 49ers were honored on the stairs of City Hall. Ray Barnett, general manager of KCBS, which broadcast the 49er games for the first time in the 1981 season, was standing at the rear of the podium and couldn't believe what he saw. "People were standing in the trees, on the top of cars, hanging out of buildings. One security guard told me he hadn't even seen anything like that in the celebrations after the war."

"On behalf of the people of the city, we would like to say welcome No. 1," said Mayor Dianne Feinstein, presenting the players and coach Bill Walsh with the symbolic keys to the city. "We have the No. 1 owner in the country, the No. 1 coach in the country, the No. 1 quarterback in the country, and the No. 1 team in the country!"

Hours before the parade for the 49ers, people started gathering along the announced parade route. Businesses let out early, out of necessity. Bus lines were rerouted because Market Street was impassable. The Bay Area Rapid Transit system carried 213,745 passengers, breaking the previous one-day record of 201,555 set the day of an American League playoff between the Oakland A's and the New York Yankees.

Motorized cable cars took the players and coaches through the financial district, but when the motorcade tried to turn from Montgomery Street onto Market Street, a wall of people blocked the way. Hundreds of screaming fans rushed toward the cable cars, wildly grabbing at the players. The cable car engines began overheating because of the slow progress, and police decided to reroute the parade two blocks away.

Anybody selling 49er memorabilia was doing a great business; at one point, a T-shirt salesman on Powell Street had 30 people waiting in line.

Marsha Washburn, a fan who came from Stockton for the parade, said of the celebration, "It's like going without sex for six months and then finally getting it."

As with the celebration the night before, there were a lot of injuries and arrests: 30 people were treated at Mission Emergency and 14 were arrested.

The biggest problem was that city officials had grossly underestimated the magnitude of the celebration. The first projections for the parade assumed that only about 20,000 people would watch.

As soon as this parade ended, police and city officials began to plan for the possibility of another one next January. Police spokesman Michael Pera said that Market Street would probably be blocked off next time, so cars and people couldn't block it themselves.

"I think even if they win next year, you're not going to get the reaction we did this year," Pera said. "Next year, people will expect them to win."

REGULAR SEASON STATISTICS

Team Statistics

	49ERS	Opp.
Time of Possession	8:27:28	7:33:30
Total First Downs	317	280
By Rushing	110	113
By Passing	183	144
By Penalty	24	23
Third Down-Made/Att..	114/259	87/224
Third Down Efficiency .	40.0%	38.8%
Total Net Yards	5484	4763
Avg Gain per Game ...	342.8	297.7
Total Offensive Plays ..	1106	1014
Avg Gain per Play	5.0	4.7
Net Yards Rushing	1941	1918
Avg Gain per Game ...	121.3	119.9
Total Rushing Plays ...	560	464
Avg Gain per Rush	3.5	4.1
Net Yards Passing	3543	2845
Avg Net Passing		
Per Game	221.4	177.8
Lost Att to Pass	29/223	36/290
Gross Yards Passing ...	3766	3135
Attempts/Completions .	517/328	514/273
Percent Complete	63.4	53.1

Had Intercepted	13	27
Punts/Average	93/41.5	83/41.4
Net Punting Average	31.1	36.0
Punt Returns/Average .	48/7.2	57/11.6
Kickoff Ret./Average ...	45/20.2	67/20.7
Intercepts/Avg Ret.....	27/16.6	13/22.8
Penalties/Yards........	92/752	108/866
Fumbles/Ball Lost	26/12	36/21
Touchdowns	43	30
By Rushing	17	10
By Passing	20	16
By Returns	6	4
Extra Points	42/43	29/30
Field Goals...........	19/29	13/23
Safeties	0	1
Total Points	357	250
Avg. Per Game	22.3	15.6

SCORE BY QUARTERS

	1	2	3	4	OT	Total
49ers Total	80	100	88	89	0	357
Opp. Total	40	76	55	79	0	250

Individual Statistics

INTRCPTNS	NO.	YDS.	AVG.	LG	TD
Hicks	9	239	26.6	72	1
Lott.........	7	117	16.7	41T	3
Williamson ..	4	44	11.0	28	0
Wright	3	26	8.7	26	0
McColl......	1	22	22.0	22	0
Reynolds....	1	0	0.0	0	0
Martin	1	0	0.0	0	0
Turner	1	0	0.0	0	0
49ERS	27	448	16.6	72	4
Opponents	13	297	22.8	101T	2

RECEIVING	NO.	YDS.	AVG.	LG	TD
Clark	85	1105	13.0	78T	4
Solomon	59	969	16.4	60T	8
Cooper	51	477	9.4	50	0
Young	37	400	10.8	29	5
Hofer	27	244	9.0	22	0
Patton	27	195	7.2	31T	1
Wilson	9	125	13.9	27T	1
Easley	9	62	6.9	21	0
Elliott	7	81	11.6	19	0
Ramson.....	4	45	11.3	16	0
Ring	3	28	9.3	21	1

	NO.	YDS.	AVG.	LG	TD
Shumann ...	3	21	7.0	8	0
Lawrence ...	3	10	3.3	5	0
Davis	3	-1	-0.3	3	0
Peets	1	5	5.0	5	0
49ERS	328	3766	11.5	78T	20
Opponents .	273	3135	11.5	67	16

RUSHING	ATT.	YDS.	AVG.	LG	TD
Patton	152	543	3.6	28	4
Cooper	98	330	3.4	23	1
Davis	94	297	3.2	14	7
Easley	76	224	2.9	9	1
Hofer	60	193	3.2	12	1
Ring	22	106	4.8	16	0
Montana	25	95	3.8	20	2
Lawrence ...	13	48	3.7	14	1
Solomon	9	43	4.8	16	0
Clark	3	32	10.7	18	0
Elliot........	7	29	4.1	9	0
Benjamin ...	1	1	1.0	1	0
49ers	560	1941	3.5	28	17
Opponents.	464	1918	4.1	29	10

SCORING	TR	TP	TRT	FG	PAT	SF	TP
Wersching	0	0	0	17-23	30-30	0	81
Solomon ..	0	8	0	0-0	0-0	0	48
Davis	7	0	0	0-0	0-0	0	42
Patton	4	1	0	0-0	0-0	0	30
Young	0	5	0	0-0	0-0	0	30
Clark	0	4	0	0-0	0-0	0	24
Bahr	0	0	0	2-6	12-12	0	18
Lott.......	0	0	3	0-0	0-0	0	18
Hicks	0	0	2	0-0	0-0	0	12
Lawrence ..	1	0	1	0-0	0-0	0	12
Montana ..	2	0	0	0-0	0-0	0	12
Cooper ...	1	0	0	0-0	0-0	0	6
Easley	1	0	0	0-0	0-0	0	6
Hofer	1	0	0	0-0	0-0	0	6
Ring	0	1	0	0-0	0-0	0	6
Wilson	0	1	0	0-0	0-0	0	6
TEAM.....	0	0	0	0-0	0-1	0	0
49ERS ...	17	20	6	19-29	42-43	0	357
Opponents	10	16	4	13-23	29-30	1	250

Kickoff Rets.	NO.	YDS.	AVG.	LG	TD
Lawrence ...	17	437	25.7	92T	1
Ring	10	217	21.7	29	0
Lott.........	7	111	15.9	20	0
Wilson	4	67	16.8	22	0
Jones	3	43	14.3	22	0
Hicks	1	22	22.0	22	0
Ramson.....	1	12	12.0	12	0
Patton	1	0	0.0	0	0
Davis	1	0	0.0	0	0
49ers	45	909	20.2	92T	1
Opponents.	67	1389	20.7	55	0

PUNT RETURNS	NO.	YDS.	AVG.	FC	LG	TD
Solomon	29	173	6.0	6	19	0
Hicks	19	171	9.0	4	39	0
49ers	48	344	7.2	10	39	0
Opponents	57	664	11.6	8	58T	0

PUNTING	NO.	YDS.	AVG.	TB	IN 20	LG	BLK
Miller	93	3858	41.5	15	14	65	0
49ers	93	3858	41.5	15	14	65	0
Opponents	83	3433	41.4	5	17	66	0

FGs.	1 -19	20 -29	30 -39	40 -49	50+	Total
Wersching	2-2	7-7	4-7	4-7	0-0	17-23
Bahr	0-0	0-2	0-1	2-3	0-0	2-6
49ers	2-2	7-9	4-8	6-10	0-0	19-29
Opponents ...	1-1	6-9	3-6	2-6	1-1	13-23

PASSING	ATT.	COMP.	YDS.	PCT.	AVG./ ATT.	TD	PCT. Td	INT.	PCT. INT.	LG	LOST/ ATT.	RATING
Montana ...	488	311	3565	63.7	7.31	19	3.9	12	2.5	78T	26/193	88.2
Benjamin ..	26	15	171	57.7	6.58	1	3.8	1	3.8	27	3/ 30	74.4
Easley	1	1	5	100.0	5.00	0	0.0	0	0.0	5	0/ 0	87.5
Clark	1	0	0	0.0	0.0	0	0.0	0	0.0	0	0/ 0	0.0
49ers	517	328	3766	63.4	7.28	20	3.9	13	2.5	78T	29/223	87.8
Opponents .	514	273	3135	53.1	6.10	16	3.1	27	5.3	67	36/290	60.0

PLAYOFF STATISTICS

Team Statistics

	49ers	Opp.
Time of Possession	52:45	1:07:15
Total First Downs	50	30
By Rushing	14	8
By Passing	30	18
By Penalty	6	4
Third Down—Made/Att	9/24	11/29
Third Down Efficiency	37.5%	37.9%
Total Net Yards	816	596
Avg. Gain per Game	408.0	298.0
Total Offensive Plays	137	121
Avg. Gain per Play	6.0	4.9
Net Yards Rushing	262	180
Avg. Gain per Game	131.0	90.0
Total Rushing Plays	65	54
Avg. Gain per Rush	4.0	3.3
Net Yards Passing	554	416
Avg. Net Passing per Game	277.0	208.0
Lost Att. to Pass	6/36	6/47
Gross Yards Passing	590	463
Attempts/Completions	66/42	61/32
Percent Complete	63.6	52.5
Had Intercepted	4	3

	49ers	Opp.
Punts/Average	8/39.1	10/41.1
Net Punting Average	35.3	34.5
Punt Returns/Average	4/11.5	6/5.2
Kickoff Ret/Average	11/18.2	12/19.3
Intercepts/Avg. Reg.	3/12.3	4/0.5
Penalties/Yards	21/251	13/100
Fumbles/Ball Lost	5/3	8/4
Touchdowns	9	6
By Rushing	3	1
By Passing	5	5
By Returns	1	0
Extra Points	9/9	6/6
Field Goals	1/2	3/4
Safeties	0	0
Total Points	66	51
Avg. per Game	33.0	25.5

Score by Quarters

	1	2	3	4	TOTAL
49ers	14	24	7	21	0-66
Opponents	17	10	7	17	0-51

Individual Statistics

RUSHING	ATT.	YDS.	AVG.	LONG	TD
Cooper	15	87	5.8	20	0
Ring	16	56	3.5	11	1
Elliott	10	48	4.8	11	0
Patton	7	32	4.6	25t	1
Solomon	2	26	13.0	14	0
Easley	6	15	2.5	5	0
Clark	1	6	6.0	6	0
Davis	2	6	3.0	4	1
Montana	6	-14	-2.3	2	0
49ers	65	262	4.0	25t	3
Opponents	54	180	3.3	13	1

RECEIVING	NO.	YDS.	AVG.	LONG	TD
Clark	13	224	17.2	39	2
Solomon	12	182	15.2	58t	2
Young	6	67	11.2	17	1
Patton	2	38	19.0	28	0
Elliott	2	29	14.5	24	0
Wilson	2	21	10.5	15	0
Cooper	2	11	5.5	6	0
Ramson	1	11	11.0	11	0
Shumann	1	11	11.0	11	0
49ers	42	590	14.0	58t	5
Opponents	32	463	14.5	72t	5

INTERCEPTIONS	NO.	YDS.	AVG.	LONG	TD
Lott	2	32	16.0	20t	1
Leopold	1	5	5.0	5	0
49ers	3	37	12.3	20t	1
Opponents	4	2	0.5	2	0

KICKOFF RTRNS	NO.	YDS.	AVG.	LONG	TD
Lawrence	6	148	24.7	47	0
Ring	4	52	13.0	17	0
Lott	1	0	0.0	0	0
49ers	11	200	18.2	47	0
Opponents	12	231	19.3	35	0

PUNT RETURNS	NO.	YDS.	AVG.	FC	LONG	TD
Solomon	2	25	12.5	1	22	0
Hicks	2	21	10.5	1	12	0
49ers	4	46	11.5	2	22	0
Opponents	6	31	5.2	0	13	0

PUNTING	NO.	YDS.	AVG.	TB	I20	LG	BK
Miller	8	313	39.1	0	2	52	0
49ers	8	313	39.1	0	2	52	0
Opponents .	10	411	41.1	1	1	51	0

FIELD GOALS	1 -19	20 -29	30 -39	40 -49	50+	TOTL
Wersching	0-0	1-1	0-0	0-0	0-1	1-2
49ers	0-0	1-1	0-0	0-0	0-1	1-2
Opponents	0-0	1-2	0-0	2-2	0-0	3-4

PASSING	ATT.	COMP.	YDS.	PCT.	AVG./ ATT.	TD	TPCT	INT.	ICPT	LG	TK/ LOST	RATING
Montana ...	66	42	590	63.6	8.94	5	7.6	4	6.1	58T	6/36	92.3
49ers	66	42	590	63.6	8.94	5	7.6	4	6.1	58T	6/36	92.3
Opponents .	61	32	463	52.5	7.59	5	8.2	3	4.9	72T	6/47	84.4

Defensive Statistics

NAME	TOTAL	TACKLES SOLO	ASSISTS	PASSES SACKS	INT.	FUMBLES DEF.	REC.	KICKS FORCED	BLOCKED
Jack Reynolds	17	9	8	0-0	0-0	1	0	1	0
Carlton Williamson	15	7	8	0-0	0-0	3	0	0	0
Archie Reese	12	7	5	0-0	0-0	0	0	0	0
Willie Harper	11	6	5	1-8	0-0	0	0	0	0
Ronnie Loft	11	8	3	0-0	2-32	2	0	0	0
Eric Wright	9	5	4	0-0	0-0	7	0	0	0
Dwight Hicks	7	4	3	0-0	0-0	1	0	0	0
Craig Puki	7	3	4	0-0	0-0	0	0	1	0
Bobby Leopold	7	4	3	0-0	1-5	1	1	0	0
Keena Turner	6	2	3	1-1	0-0	0	1	0	0
Lawrence Pillers	4	3	1	2-20	0-0	1	0	1	0
Fred Dean	3	1	3	0-0	0-0	0	0	0	0
Dan Bunz	4	2	2	0-0	0-0	0	0	0	0
Mike Wilson	3	2	1	0-0	0-0	0	0	0	0
Dwaine Board	3	1	2	1-11	0-0	1	0	0	0
Milt McColl	3	1	2	0-0	0-0	0	0	0	0
Amos Lawrence	2	2	0	0-0	0-0	0	1	0	0
Lynn Thomas	2	2	0	0-0	0-0	1	0	0	0
Jim Stuckey	2	1	1	1-7	0-0	1	0	0	0
Rick Gervais	1	1	0	0-0	0-0	0	0	0	0
Fred Solomon	1	1	0	0-0	0-0	0	0	0	0
John Harty	1	1	0	0-0	0-0	0	0	0	0
Ricky Patton	1	1	0	0-0	0-0	0	0	0	0
Ray Wersching	1	0	1	0-0	0-0	0	0	0	0

DIRECTORY

Management

Edward DeBartolo, Jr. .... President
Franklin Mieuli .... Limited Partner
Mrs. Victor P. Morabito .... Limited Partner

Administrative Staff

John McVay .... Director of Football Operations
Ken Flower... Director of Marketing & Community Affairs
Keith Simon .... Business Manager
George Heddleston .... Director of Public Relations
Jerry Walker .... Assistant Director of Public Relations
Delia Newland... Assistant Director of Publicity
Ted Glarrow.. Ticket Manager
Ken Dargel... Assistant Ticket Manager
R. C. Owens .... Executive Assistant
Melrene Frear .... Controller
Roy Gilbert .... Film Director
Walt Porep ....Game Films Photographer
Michael Zagaris
Dennis Desprois... Photographers
Michael Olmstead .... Entertainment Director
Chris Poehler,
Paul Potyen .... Band Directors
S. Dan Brodie .... Statistician
Chico Norton ....Equipment Manager
Don Klein
Wayne Walker .... 49ers' Radio
Greg Cosmos,
Ted Walsh .... Assistant Equipment Managers

Coaching Staff

Bill Walsh ....General Manager-Head Coach
Chuck Studley .... Defensive Coordinator
Norb Hecker .... Linebackers
Milt Jackson .... Special Teams – Receivers
Billie Matthews .... Running Backs
Bobb McKittrick .... Offensive Line
Bill McPherson .... Defensive Line
George Seifert .... Secondary
Al Vermeil... Strength and Conditioning
Sam Wyche .... Quarterbacks
Cas Banaszek ....Assistant Offensive Line
Ray Rhodes .... Assistant Secondary

Scouting Staff

Tony Razzano.. Director of College Scouting
Proverb Jacobs... Pro Scouting
Vic Lindskog .... Scout
Ernie Plank .... Scout
Warren Schmakel.. Scout
Neil Schmidt .... Scout
Billy Wilson .... Scout
Neal Dahlen.. Staff Assistant

AMERICA HAS A BETTER TEAM

The Remarkable Story of Bill Walsh and San Francisco's Super Bowl Champion 49ers

By Glenn Dickey
Introduction by Herb Caen
Kind words by Mayor Dianne Feinstein

"You just beat America's team." (Too Tall Jones to Joe Montana after the latter's game winning throw in the historic Dallas-49er confrontation January 10, 1982.)

America has a *better* team—the amazing San Francisco 49ers. Now the San Francisco Chronicle's irascible sportswriter Glenn Dickey recreates their exciting story in the first book to be published on the subject: *America Has A Better Team: The Remarkable Story of Bill Walsh and San Francisco's Super Bowl Champion 49ers.*

It's all here: the lean years with Morabito, the purchase by the DeBartolos, the hiring of Bill Walsh, the building of the world champion team. We relive the golden season game by game, witness the growing support of the fans until the finale when all San Francisco takes to the streets in jubilation. As Herb Caen points out, the 49ers' story is not just the story of a football team but of the restoration of the ego of a beleagured city.

The author of eight other books and over 70 magazine articles, Glenn Dickey brings his extensive knowledge of pro football and of the 49ers in particular to the telling of *America Has A Better Team.*

Discounts of 30% and over are available for bulk purchases.

"AMERICA HAS A BETTER TEAM"
Use the specialized order form below to order copies now!

- -

YES! Please send me the following order of AMERICA HAS A BETTER TEAM.

_____ copies of the trade paperback edition ($9.95, ISBN 0-936602-47)

_____ copies of the hardcover edition ($14.95, ISBN 0-936602-48-1)

_____ copies of the limited hardcover edition ($25.00, ISBN 0-936602-49)

_____ Discount

_____ Total amount of order

Name _____Company _____

Address _____

City_____State _____Zip _____

Return orders to: Harbor Publishing, Inc., 1668 Lombard St.,
Dept. CT, 1668 Lombard St., San Francisco, CA 94123